PRAXIS, TRUTH, AND LIBERATION

Essays on Gadamer, Taylor, Polanyi, Habermas, Gutierrez, and Ricoeur

Terry Hoy, Ph.D.
Simpson College

UNIVERSITY
PRESS OF
AMERICA

Lanham • New York • London

British Cataloging in Publication Information Available

Library of Congress Cataloging-in-Publication Data

Hoy, Terry.
Praxis, truth, and liberation.

Includes index.
1. Hermeneutics—History—20th century. 2. Liberty—
History—20th century. 3. Knowledge, Theory of.
4. Phenomenology—History—20th century. I. Title.
BD241.H75   1988   190'.9'04   88–17259
ISBN 0–8191–7072–0 (pbk. : alk. paper)

All University Press of America books are produced on acid-free paper.
The paper used in this publication meets the minimum requirements of American
National Standard for Information Sciences—Permanence of Paper for Printed
Library Materials, ANSI Z39.48–1984.

ACKNOWLEDGMENTS

Grateful acknowledgment is made to the following publishers for permission to reprint articles by the author from their publications:

Hoy, Terry. "Michael Polanyi: The Moral Imperatives of a Free Society." Thought (December 1983) reprinted by permission of Fordham University Press.

Hoy, Terry. "Gustavo Gutierrez: Latin American Liberation Theology." International Journal of Social Economics. Vol. 13, no. 9 (1986) reprinted by permission of MCB University Press Limited.

Table of Contents

INTRODUCTION

The concept of praxis and its relationship to truth and human liberation has become a prominent theme in both contemporary philosophy and theology. Such figures as Hans Gadamer, Charles Taylor, Paul Ricoeur, and Richard Rorty have been among the more influential expressions of a hermeneutical philosophy rejecting the ahistorical, objectivist criteria of truth and morality associated with the Cartesian-Kantian heritages and emphasizing the centrality of the interpretive understanding of texts, historical practice, and traditions. From the standpoint of the philosophy of science, Thomas Kuhn has been an influential spokesman of the view that scientific inquiry does not proceed by objective criteria of verification and experimentation but by "paradigm" constructions that are the product of traditions of scientific research. Changes from one paradigm to another are not the result of the logic of experiment alone, but rather seeing things from a different point of view that is equivalent to a faith commitment or a "conversion" experience. Michael Polanyi has articulated a concept of "personal knowledge" that challenges the objectivist criteria of verification that has been the hallmark of scientific positivism, his contention that scientific inquiry embodies a dimension of personal knowledge that transcends the disjunction between objective and subjective, reason vs. faith, fact, and value, a knowledge that encompasses a tacit or subsidiary awareness analogous to a skill or connoisseurship.

An orientation to the understanding of the meaning of freedom and liberation is also a central focus of contemporary forms of praxis interpretation. The concept of moral agency and personhood is a central theme in the hermeneutical interpretation of Charles Taylor. Polanyi's concept of personal knowledge embodies the contention that the values of a democratic society (civil liberties, free inquiry, the pursuit of truth and justice) constitute the premises of all forms of personal knowing, both scientific and humanistic. The more radical implications of praxis analysis have been articulated by Jurgen Habermas: a critical social theory as a protest against the dominance of technique in modern industrial society, an emphasis on Marxist critique of ideology and Freudian psychoanalysis as forms of rationality that can facilitate the task of human emancipation. In his more recent writings

Habermas has sought to articulate the concept of a communicative rationality, in opposition to the purposive rationality of technical means and efficiency, as the basis for intersubjective recognition of validity claims in an ideal speech situation, freed from inner and outer restraints, directed to truth, freedom, and justice.

In the area of theological reflection, the concept of liberation praxis has been given its most influential expression by Gustavo Gutierrez. Classical theology, wisdom, and knowledge, he contends, must not be ignored, but historical praxis must be the point of departure for theological reflection, and historical praxis is liberation praxis in identification with oppressed classes and solidarity with their interests and struggles. While Gutierrez appropriates conventional Marxist categories in his view of Latin American historical realities, he has been little influenced by the revisionist Marxist focus upon problems of technical domination and control peculiar to Western industrial societies and even less by the turn to linguistic analysis central to Habermas' theory of communicative rationality. But liberation theology bears a strong affinity to the critical theory of Habermas as a general reaction against the classical subordination of praxis to theory, and the general contention that praxis interpretation must be identified with human emancipation and liberation.

While a praxis orientation is a widely shared emphasis in both contemporary philosophy and theology, there are significant variations and contrast among its leading exponents, particularly at two key dimensions. One would be a contrast in terms of the implications of hermeneutical interpretation in relation to general criteria of normative judgment and evaluation. Positions represented by such figures as Gadamer, Habermas, Ricoeur, and Taylor, while sharing a common reaction against objectivist, ahistorical standards of Enlightenment rationalism,would seek to sustain the possibility of truth claims or normative universals within the framework of hermeneutical interpretation. But the more radical forms of historicism or so-called deconstructivism, such as the position represented by Richard Rorty, would reject any possibility for normative criteria beyond the contingencies of specific historical practices and conventions. In the view of Rorty,reconstructive efforts such as that of Gadamer or Habermas would be seen as a perpetuation of the same mistakes of the past in attempts to establish basic foundations or constraints.

A second dimension of disagreement would be between the "hermeneutics of tradition" associated with Habermas vs. the "critique of ideology" associated with Habermas. Central to Gadamer's hermeneutical interpretation is the defense of prejudice, authority, and tradition against the presuppositions of Enlightenment rationalism. While Gadamer argues that his concept of hermeneutical reason is not simply a conservative traditionalism or that it denies the importance of critical reflection, he insists that there is no social reality that does not bring itself to representation in a consciousness that is linguistically mediated. Habermas agrees with Gadamer's emphasis upon the need for hermeneutical interpretation in opposition to scientific positivism, and he agrees that hermeneutical insight cannot leap over the interpreter's relation to tradition. But Habermas contends that Gadamer's emphasis upon tradition and language ties itself to idealist presuppositions that linguistically articulated conscience determines material life. Such an approach to hermeneutical interpretation, he believes, fails to recognize that the linguistic infrastructure of society may also be intertwined with frozen relations of power and domination. It is for this reason that a "critique of ideology" is necessary to release the subject from a dependency on "hypostatized powers," and as a basis for the achievement of a communicative action freed from external and internal constraints.

Despite differences and contrasts within the spectrum of praxist interpretation, it is possible to discern potentialities for an integrative perspective. It is the intent of this study to explore this potential through a critical examination of representatives of praxis interpretation who, in varying ways, embody constructive possibilities for truth claims and normative universals within the framework of hermeneutical interpretation. In the case of Gadamer this involves a contention that hermeneutical interpretation is a basis for "fusion of horizons," as well as a contention that human language is the basis for a common life in which man is able to make distinctions of moral worth and value. Taylor, in similar terms, emphasizes the concept of "self interpretation" linked to the role of language as basis for emotions and feelings of dignity, guilt, moral obligations, and so forth that are intrinsic to the domain of what it is to be fully human. Polanyi argues for a concept of personal knowledge that challenges the dualisms of subjective vs. objective, fact vs. value, reason vs. faith fostered by scientific positivism. He also argues that the values of democratic society (civil liberties, free inquiry, the pursuit of truth and justice) constitutes the premises of all forms of personal knowing both scientific and humanistic. Habermas seeks to establish a basis for a communicative rationality as the consensus-bringing argumentative speech in which participants overcome merely subjective views, assuring themselves of the unity of the objective world and the intersubjectivity of their "lifeworld." Ricoeur shares with Gadamer the general postulates of a hermeneutical ontology, but also contributes to a hermeneutics of symbolism focusing upon human consciousness of guilt and evil, a biblical hermeneutics of "freedom in the light of hope," and a philosophical approximation to the Kerygma in the Kantian concept of practical reason.

The contention that the above representatives of hermeneutical interpretation are the more hopeful prospects for the achievement of an integrative perspective would, thus, be in basic opposition to the central thesis of Richard Bernstein in his widely acclaimed and influential book, Beyond Objectivism and Relativism. Bernstein believes that the tangled controversies that have grown up between objectivism vs. relativism relate to a "Cartesian anxiety," the conclusion to which Descartes leads us as a grand and seductive "either/or"--either there is some support for our being, a fixed foundation for knowledge, or we cannot escape intellectual chaos. Bernstein is convinced that this dichotomy is misleading and distortive and that we need to "exorcise the Cartesian anxiety" and liberate ourselves from its seductive appeal. This leads Bernstein to conclude that the best direction beyond objectivism and relativism is in terms of a common ground between Habermas, Gadamer, and Rorty: the concept of open conversational dialogue rather than any hope for consensus in regard to truth claims or criteria of normative validation or justification.

It is the contention of this study, in opposition to Bernstein, that conversational dialogue, although obviously basic to a concept of freedom and liberation, entails ontological presuppositions having to do with human agency and personhood, and human language as a mode of being in the world, which a hermeneutical interpretation must seek to clarify. It is for this reason that positions represented by such figures as Gadamer, Taylor, and Ricoeur cannot be seen simply as common ground with Rorty but rather as an opposition to the radical historical relativism and nihilist implications that Rorty's deconstructivism inevitably entails. This would not deny the general spirit of Bernstein's contention that reconstructive efforts must move in a direction beyond objectivism and relativism; but it will be the intent of this study to argue that positions represented by Taylor, Polanyi, Gadamer, Ricoeur, and Habermas embody constructive possibilities for sustaining the possibility of normative criteria and truth claims without falling into philosophical absolutism or dogmatism.

In regard to the meaning of praxis interpretation in relationship to human liberation, it will be the intent to defend the critical theory of Habermas as a focus upon the problem of emancipation from technical domination and manipulation in modern industrial society, and Gutierrez's liberation theology as a focus upon the meaning of liberation praxis in the context of Third World social injustice and oppression. But it will also be emphasized that in his debate with Habermas, Gadamer has provided a persuasive case that his "hermeneutic of tradition" is not simply a conservative apologetic; that the historicity of the knower does not impair the role of critical reflection; and that there is a point of constructive dialogue between a hermeneutic of tradition and a critique of ideology.

Finally, it will be the intent to show that the writings of Paul Ricoeur provide a framework for the integration of philosophical and theological hermeneutics in relationship to liberation praxis: a hermeneutical ontology convergent with the position of Gadamer, but also a biblical hermeneutic of "freedom in light of hope," and a philosophical approximation to Kerygma in the Kantian concept of practical reason. Ricoeur's hermeneutical phenomenology also involves an attempt to arbitrate between Gadamer's "hermeneutic of tradition" and Habermas' "critique of ideology." In his political essays Ricoeur provides a critique of problems of objectification and alienation in modern industrial society that converges with the critical theory of Habermas, and an emphasis upon the relevance of Christian love to the sphere of social action on behalf of the poor and oppressed that converges with the central themes of liberation theology.

CHAPTER 1

THE HERMENEUTICS OF HANS GADAMER:
TOWARDS THE RENEWAL OF ARISTOTELIAN PRAXIS

Hans Gadamer has been one of the more
influential figures in contemporary hermeneutical
interpretation as a critical reaction against the
objectivist, ahistorical presuppositions of
Enlightenment rationalism, and as an emphasis upon the
historical, linguistic character of human
understanding. What is of singular importance in
Gadamer's contribution is the contention that the concept of Aristotelian praxis and phronesis constitutes
a model for hermeneutical interpretation as an
approach to defining the relationship of universals to
particular situations; the distinction between scientific, technical knowledge as opposed to the practical
prudential wisdom involved in moral action and
governance.

Whether a concept of hermeneutical interpretation,
as the appropriation of Aristotelian praxis, can be
given relevance to the contemporary historical period
is, of course, controversial and problematical. One
critical objection most forcefully articulated by
Jurgen Habermas is that Gadamer's "hermeneutics of
tradition" embodies a conservative apologetic that
fails to recognize the need for critical reflection
directed against institutional reification and
answering the human interest in emancipation. A
second objection raised by Richard Bernstein is that
Gadamer fails to confront the fact that we are living
in times in which the basic presuppositions of
Aristotelian praxis (the shared meanings and values
of a common life) no longer exist. A third objection
stems from the radical antifoundationalist type of
hermeneutical interpretation (given most influential
expression by Richard Rorty) that Aristotle's concept
of praxis cannot be divorced from metaphysical aspects
of his thought that are no longer credible in the
modern age.

It is the general contention of this essay,
however, that Gadamer provides a convincing articulation of a general hermeneutical theory in relationship
to the concept of Aristotelian praxis, and that this
position can be effectively defended against the above
objections. This will entail the contention that in a

rejoinder to Habermas, Gadamer convincingly argues
that his hermeneutical theory does not constitute a
reification of tradition in opposition to critical
reflection. The breakdown of normative consensus in
the modern era, it will also be argued, does not mean
the absence of historical tendencies that can sustain
the relevance of the concept of Aristotelian praxis in
the context of modern constitutional democracy.
Finally, it will be argued that Gadamer provides an
interpretation of Aristotelian logos as the human
capacity for language rather than human mind as a
correspondence with external reality. Such an
interpretation avoids the errors of an objectivist
epistemology and provides a constructive move in the
direction of a hermeneutical ontology beyond the
polarities of metaphysical absolutism as well as
historical relativism and nihilism.

I

In viewing Gadamer's hermeneutical theory as a
defense of historical consciousness and tradition
against the presuppositions of Enlightenment rationalism, it would be important to emphasize that Gadamer
is not defending the romantic school of nineteenth
century historicism: "the romantic faith in the
growth of tradition before which reason must remain
silent is just as prejudiced and is fundamentally like
the Enlightenment."[1] Gadamer contends that tradition
is constantly an element of freedom and history
itself. Even the most genuine and solid tradition
does not persist simply because of the inertia of
what once existed. "It needs to be affirmed,
enhanced, and cultivated.... Preservation is as much a
freely chosen action as revolution and renewal....
That is why both the Enlightenment critique of tradition and its romantic rehabilitation is less than
their true historical being."[2]

At the very beginning of historical hermeneutics,
Gadamer asserts, the antithesis between history and
knowledge must be discarded. The effect of living
tradition and the effect of historical study must
constitute a unity and a texture of reciprocal
relationship.[3]

Gadamer emphasizes the concept of a "hermeneutical
circle," neither subjective nor objective but the
interplay of the movement of tradition and the movement of interpretation. The meaning that governs our
interpretation of the text is not an act of subjec-

tivity but forms a sense of community that binds us to a tradition. But tradition is not simply a precondition into which we come. We produce it ourselves insofar as we understand and participate in the evolution of a tradition.[4]

Gadamer also emphasizes that time is no longer a gulf to be bridged, which was the naive assumption of historicism--the view that we must set ourselves in the spirit of the age. In fact, distance in time is a productive and positive possibility as the recognition of continuity of custom and tradition in which all that is handed down presents itself to us.[5] Gadamer speaks of the principle of "effective history," recognizing that we are always within a situation, an essential point of which is a concept of "horizon," a range of vision that includes everything that can be seen from a particular standpoint. The historical movement of life is never utterly bound to any one standpoint; there is never a truly closed horizon. Placing historical consciousness within a historical horizon does not mean passing into an alien world unconnected with our own. There is, in fact, a single horizon that embraces everything contained in historical consciousness. The horizons of the present cannot be formed without the past; understanding is always a "fusion of horizons." Every encounter with tradition that takes place within historical consciousness involves the experience of tension between the text and the present. The hermeneutical task is not covering up this tension by attempting a naive assimilation but consciously bringing it out where old and new continually grow together "making something of living value without either being explicitly distinguished from the other."[6]

Gadamer believes that hermeneutical understanding in regard to the problem of the relationship of universals to particulars gives Aristotle's ethics a special importance. Gadamer recognizes that Aristotle was not concerned with the hermeneutical problem of the historical dimension but rather with the role of "right reason" in moral action. But Aristotle is concerned with reason and knowledge as part of a being that is becoming. Aristotle's inquiry, in this sense, is detached from the intellectuality of Plato and Socrates. Aristotle thus becomes the foundation of ethics independent of metaphysics. Criticizing the Platonic idea of the good, Aristotle asks the question of the good, not as an empty generalization but as the good in terms of human action. Aristotle

believed that the equating of virtue with knowledge in
Plato and Socrates in an exaggeration. For Aristotle,
human civilization differs essentially from nature in
that man becomes what he is through what he does and
how he behaves--where we have to do with institutions
that can be changed and that have the quality of rules
only to a limited degree.[7]

In Aristotle's ethics the knowledge that cannot be
applied to the concrete situation becomes meaningless
and risks obscuring the demands that the situation
makes. Gadamer employs Aristotle's distinction between knowledge of phronesis and theoretical knowledge
of episteme. The latter is the mode of mathematics,
unchangeable and amenable to proof that can be known
by anyone. But the knowledge of phronesis is the
knowledge of man as an acting being concerned with
what is not always the same as it is but can also be
different; "the purpose of his knowledge is to govern
action."[8]

Nor can moral judgment be the same as the
craftsman in that we possess knowledge in such a way
that we already have it and then apply it to a specific situation. While one has guiding ideas of right
and wrong (decency, courage, dignity, and so on),
there is a basic difference from the guiding ideas
represented by the plan the craftsman has of an object
he is is going to make. What is right cannot be determined independently of the situation that requires a
right action from me, whereas the idea of what a
craftsman desires to make is fully determined by the
use for which it is intended. It would be true, to
be sure, that the administration of justice requires
the application of laws and rules to a specific content analogous with the craftsman. But in the case of
a person applying the law, the full rigor of the law
may have to be modified. Everything that is set down
in the law is in a necessary tension with a definite
action and cannot contain within itself practical
reality in its full concrete form.[9]

Aristotle's concept of natural law is not to be
equated with the modern expression. While he accepts
the ideal of an absolutely unchangeable law, this is
limited to the gods, but among men, legal and natural
law can be changed. In view of the necessary imper-
fections of all human laws, the ideal of natural law
is indispensable for Aristotle particularly in
questions of equity. But its function is a critical
one in that the appeal to natural law is legitimate

only where a discrepancy emerges between one law and
another. Ideas of what man ought to be (as bravery)
are not just arbitrary conventions but have to be made
in concrete situations of the person acting. This
requires a fundamental modification between means and
ends that distinguishes moral from technical
knowledge. Even if we conceive of moral knowledge as
an ideal perfection, it is a perfection that requires
self-deliberation and not knowledge in the manner of
technique. Moral knowledge can never be known in
advance as a knowledge that can be taught.
Aristotle's theory of virtue describes typical forms
of the true mean that it is important to observe in
human life and behavior in response to demands of the
situation of the moment.[10]

A further quality of moral knowledge besides <u>phro-
nesis</u> is the understanding that has to do with concern, not about oneself, but about the other person;
where we place ourselves in concrete situations in
which the other person has to act. This is not in any
sense a technical knowledge, but the understanding of
one who is seeking what is right united with the
other person in mutual interest. A concrete example of
this is advice on questions of conscience where both
the person who asks for advice and the person giving
it assume the other is a friend. "The person with
understanding does not know and judge as one who
stands apart and is unaffected but as one who is
united by a specific bond with another, he thinks with
the other and undergoes the situation with him."[11]

Aristotle's analysis, Gadamer concludes, is a
model for hermeneutics where application is integral
to understanding and not the relation of a pregiven
universal to a particular situation.

> The interpreter dealing with a traditional
> text seeks to apply it to himself. But this
> does not mean that the text is given to him
> as something universal, that he understands
> it as such and only afterwards uses it for
> particular applications. Rather, the
> interpreter seeks no more than to understand
> this universal thing, the text, i.e., to
> understand what this piece of tradition
> says, what constitutes the meaning and impor-
> tance of the text. In order to understand
> that, he must not seek to disregard himself
> and his particular hermeneutical situation.
> He must relate the text to this situation,
> if he wants to understand it at all.[12]

5

Because of his emphasis upon the centrality of text or tradition in opposition to the presuppositions of Enlightenment rationalism, Gadamer has been subject to the charge that his hermeneutical interpretation lends itself to conservative political implications. This contention has been most forcefully articulated by Jurgen Habermas.

While sharing Gadamer's emphasis upon the need for hermeneutical interpretation in opposition to the narrow strictures of scientific positivism and technological rationality, Habermas emphasizes the need for critical reflection as the basis for emancipation from oppressive social structures and traditions. Hermeneutical insight, he would agree, cannot leap over the interpreter's relationship to tradition, but it does not follow from this that tradition cannot be profoundly altered by scientific reflection. Gadamer, he believes, fails to recognize that language is dependent upon social processes not reducible to normative relationships, where language serves to legitimize relations of organized force. Language, thus, becomes ideological, originating not only from systems of domination but from social labor and from the institutional structures of science and technology.

While these structures are linguistically mediated, they also indirectly exercise an influence on the linguistic sphere. A sociology that hypostatizes language and forms of life and tradition, Habermas contends, ties itself to idealist assumptions that linguistically articulated conscience determines material practices of society. Habermas emphasizes the constraints of an "outer nature" that enters into the procedures for technical mastery, and an "inner nature" reflecting the oppressive character of social power structures. "Social action can only be constituted in an objective framework that is constituted conjointly by language, labor, and domination."[13]

The critique of Habermas points up difficulties in Gadamer's hermeneutics that would be apparent from his primary work, Truth and Method, but in subsequent response to Habermas' criticism, Gadamer has provided a clarification that is persuasive in showing that his concept of hermeneutical reason does not imply a bias in favor of conservative traditionalism or that it fails to recognize the importance of critical reflection. Gadamer is quite willing to concede the view of

Habermas that there are levels of reality that are not of a linguistic order. The cultural heritage, he concedes, involves forms of techniques and domination, of ideals of liberty and objective possibilities that do not subsist solely in language. Nor does he deny that social structures and processes embody dogmatic power and authority, from the ordering of education and the mandatory commands of the army and government all the way to the hierarchy of power created by political forces of fanatics.[14]

But Gadamer challenges the view of Habermas that there are so-called "real factors" such as work or politics that are outside the scope of hermeneutics. While hermeneutical understanding does not mean that a cultural tradition should be absolutized or fixed, it does mean that we should try to understand everything that can be understood. The world of meaning, he contends, cannot be narrowed down to the status of secondary objects of knowledge and mere supplements to the economic and political realities that fundamentally determine the life of society. The mirror of language is the reflection of everything that is. "In language, and only in it, can we meet what we never encounter in the world, because we are ourselves (and not merely what we mean or what we know of ourselves)." But the metaphor of a mirror is not fully adequate to the phenomenon of language, for in the last analysis, language is not simply a mirror.

> What we perceive in it is not merely a
> reflection of our own and all being; it
> is the living out of what it is with us--
> not only in all other interrelationships
> of work and politics, but in all the
> other relationships and dependencies that
> comprise our world.[15]

Gadamer does not wish to contend that linguistically articulated consciousness claims to determine all the material being of life practice. But there is no societal reality with all its concrete forces that does not bring itself to representation in a consciousness that is linguistically articulated.

> Reality does not happen behind the back of
> language; it happens rather behind the backs
> of those who live in the subjective opinion
> that they have understood the world (or can
> no longer understand it), that is, reality
> happens precisely within language.[16]

7

Gadamer does not see hermeneutical interpretation in opposition to the importance of critical reflection. The fact that it is in the midst of a linguistic world and through the mediation of an experience preformed by language that we grow up in our world does not remove the possibilities of critique.

On the contrary, the possibility of going beyond our conventions and beyond all those experiences that are schematized in advance, opens up before us once we find ourselves, in our conversation with others, faced with opposed thinkers with new critical problems, with new experiences. Fundamentally in our world the issue is always the same: the verbalization of conventions and of social norms behind which there are always economic and dominating interests. But our human experience of the world, for which we rely on our faculty of judgment, consists precisely in the possibility of our taking a critical stance with regard to every convention. In reality, we owe this to the linguistic virtuality of our reason and language does not, therefore, present an obstacle to reason.[17]

Gadamer emphasizes that language is not the anonymous subject of all sociohistorical processes that would present the whole of its activities as objectivations to our observing gaze. It is rather a game of interpretation in which we all participate, where everyone takes a turn and where understanding is especially in seeing through prejudice or pretenses that hide reality. But Gadamer contends that we do not understand only when we see through pretexts or false pretensions (which the Marxist perspective of Habermas seems to presuppose). Reflection is not always an unavoidable step towards dissolving prior convictions. Authority is not always wrong. In Habermas, authority is by definition a dogmatic power. But Gadamer does not agree to a view of reason and authority as an abstract antithesis as did the emancipatory Enlightenment. While authority can be associated with innumerable forms of domination and where the mere outward appearance of obedience cannot be a basis for legitimation, it is the acceptance or acknowledgment that is decisive for relationships of authority. Authority can only rule when it is recognized and accepted; "the obedience that belongs to true authority is neither blind nor slavish."[18]

What emerges from the debate between Gadamer and
Habermas are significant implications that lead in the
direction of an integrative perspective. Gadamer is
not denying that there are levels of reality having to
do with techniques of power and domination that are
not of a linguistic order, and he is not denying the
need for a critical reflection that would serve human
interest in emancipation and liberation. But what he
rightfully objects to is that one can understand
social realities independently from the dimension of
hermeneutical interpretation or what finally brings
itself to representations that are linguistically
mediated.

Paul Ricoeur's analysis of the debate between
Gadamer and Habermas (which will be given more
detailed discussion in the concluding chapter)helps to
put into a balanced perspective the problem of the
relationship between a "hermeneutic of tradition" and
a "critique of ideology." The interest in emancipation, he contends, would be empty and abstract if
it were not situated on the same place as historical
hermeneutical sciences, that is, at the level of communicative action. "The task of a hermeneutic of tradition" is to remind the "critique of ideology" that
man can project his emancipation and anticipate an
unlimited and unconstrained communication only the
basis of the creative interpretation of a cultural
heritage.[19] Ricoeur does not wish to deny a difference between "hermeneutics of tradition" and the
"critique of ideology": the one a theory of the text,
the other an analysis of institutions and the phenomena of reifications and alienations. "But it is the
task of philosophical reflection to eliminate decep-
tive antinomies which would oppose the interest in the
reinterpretation of a cultural heritage received from
the past and the interest in the futuristic projections of a liberated humanity."[20]

III

A second critical reaction to Gadamer's hermeneutical theory, as an appropriation of Aristotelian
praxis, centers upon the question of its relevance to
the political context of modernity. Richard Bernstein
in his book Beyond Objectivism and Relativism takes
Gadamer to task on this point. Given a community in
which there is a shared acceptance of ethical principles and norms, Aristotle's concept of praxis as the
mediation of universals in concrete situations makes
sense.

But what becomes so problematical for us today, what is characteristic of our hermeneutical situation, is that there is so much confusion and uncertainty (some might even say chaos) about what are the norms or universals which ought to govern our practical lives. What Gadamer himself realizes--but I do not think he squarely faces the issues that it raises--is that we are living in a time when the very conditions required for the exercise of phronesis--the shared accceptance and stability of universal principles and laws--are themselves breaking down.[21]

Bernstein's emphasis upon the alienation of modernity from the normative framework of Greek polis is well founded. But it is not accurate to say that this is an issue that Gadamer does not squarely face. For he is fully cognizant of the forces of modernity that impede the possibility of a hermeneutic as a practical philosophy having to do with what is each individual's due as a citizen and what constitutes his arete or excellence. Instead, we have the ascendency of a criteria of technological efficiency where the expert becomes the substitute for practical experience, where we witness the technologizing of the formation of public opinion, the degeneration of practice into technique, and a general decline into social irrationality.[22]

Whether Aristotelian praxis can any longer be seen as relevant to the context of modernity is, of course, problematical. Gadamer speculates that there may be hope for renewal of the normative character of practical reason due to a growing consciousness of the fatal path down which humanity is heading and of the limits of human control and manipulation; the revulsion against brainwashing, genetic breeding, and the postponement of death; the increasing awareness of the ecological crisis that confronts our planet; the "shuddering thought" that we have a type of democracy that depends upon the photogenic qualities of the presidency.[23]

But perhaps the more positive case that can be made for the contemporary relevance of Aristotelian praxis is the element of continuity of modernity with a classical heritage that, in the American experience, has been well documented by Robert Bellah. The Puritan heritage, he points out, was the attempt to combine Christian charity with civic virtue, a social, communal emphasis derived from the classical ideal of polis, the Old Testament covenant between God and people and the New Testament notion of community based on charity and love.[24] The Founding Fathers were also influenced by the classical political philosophers from Aristotle to Montesquieu who saw in the political regime the embodiment of Republican concepts of representation, participation in the exercise of power, the equality of citizens, and the willingness to subordinate private interest to the common good. The Revolutionary period and the Civil War, Bellah contends, were trial periods in which classical ideas were given their most notable expression.[25]

Bellah recognizes that the practical utilitarianism of the Lockean tradition associated with the rise of commercial capitalism has become a pervasive ethos of American political consciousness: a technical, regulative conception of political society in which the state is seen as a neutral arbiter among competing interests out of which it is assumed the general interest will emerge.[26] But it is Bellah's thesis that elements of the classical heritage are still present in contemporary political consciousness. Reformist movements of the modern era such as populism, the progressive movement, the New Deal, and the civil rights movement, while mixed with individualist-utilitarian values, embodied concepts of equality, social justice, and human community that can be seen in continuity with classical virtues. In more recent years the growing ecological consciousness and the peace and social justice orientation of the Church can be seen as a continuing emphasis upon the subordination of individualist egoism and self-interests to human community and the common good.[27]

One can well agree with Bernstein on the difficulties of seeking to establish the relevance of the classical tradition to the context of modernity, and that the principal task of political theory is to show how this transformation came about and what to do about it. But such a task cannot be a question of assuming that the context of modernity constitutes a total break from the classical tradition.

Gadamer's hermeneutical interpretation correctly reminds us that confrontation with problems of the present is always within the consciousness of a tradition that addresses us. The horizon of the present cannot be formed without the past. Understanding is a

11

"fusion of horizons" in which every encounter with tradition takes place within historical consciousness, an experience of tension between the traditional text and the present. The hermeneutical task is not covering up this tension by attempting a naive assimilation but consciously bringing it out, where the old and the new grow together making something of living value without either being explicitly distinct from the other. Gadamer's attempt to provide relevance of the concept of Aristotelian praxis within the framework of hermeneutical interpretation thus provides a significant contribution to the contemporary task of sustaining the continuity of the classical ideal of political philosophy with problems of the present.

IV

Perhaps the most controversial aspect of Gadamer's hermeneutical theory is its implication as a truth claim that can be sustained as an alternative to inadequacies of classical metaphysics as well as the objectivist criteria of Enlightenment rationalism. It is Aristotle, Gadamer contends, who established the classical definition of man according to which man is a living being who has logos. The tradition of the East and the canonical forms of this definition, he points out, have been animal rationale--man as the rational being distinguished from other animals by his capacity for thought. But, in Gadamer's view, the primary meaning of logos is language. Animals can understand each other by indicating to each other what excites their desire so they can seek it, or what injures them so they can flee it. But for man alone is language given so that people can manifest to each other what is right and wrong. Man, as an individual, has logos; he can think and speak; he can communicate what he means. And it is by virtue of this fact that among men there can be a common life without murder or manslaughter, a political constitution and an organized division of labor. "All this is involved in the simple assertion that man is a being who possesses language."[28]

The centrality of language, Gadamer contends, has been overshadowed by the Cartesian characterization of conscience and self-conscience, which became the standard for meeting the requirements of scientific knowledge in the modern period. Gadamer emphasizes that language is not simply one of the means by which consciousness is mediated in the world; it is not simply a third instrument alongside signs and tools

12

both of which are also distinctively human. For we never find ourselves as consciousness over against the world; in our knowledge of ourselves and the world, we are already encompassed by language that is our own-- the acquiring of a familiarity with the world and how it confronts us. It is through language, as Aristotle realized, that one comes to recognize universals, the capacity for meaning that allows us to recognize something as the same and that is the first great achievement of abstraction. We are always biased in our thinking and knowledge by our linguistic interpretation of the world. To grow into linguistic interpretation is to grow up into the world. Logos is the real mark of our finitude; it is always before us; the consicousness of the individual is not the standard by which the being of language can be measured.[29]

Gadamer believes that it is possible to distinguish three things that are peculiar to language. One is an essential "self-forgetfulness." The structure of grammar and syntax are not at all conscious to living speaking; its real being consists in what is said in it, a common world in which we live, which belongs to the great chain of tradition reaching us from literature and foreign language, living and dead.[30]

A second feature of language is its "I-lessness." To speak means to speak to someone; speaking does not belong to the sphere of I but We. The operation of dialogue can be seen in the spirit of the "game" from the point of view of the conscience of the player. The game is a dynamic process that embraces the persons playing. The attitude of players is not an attitude of subjectivity; rather it is the game itself that plays, drawing the players into itself.[31]

A third feature is the universality of language. It is all encompassing; nothing is excluded from being said, keeping pace with the universality of reason. Nothing that is said has its truth simply in itself but instead refers backward and forward to what is unsaid. There is an infinite dialogue in question and answers in whose space word and answers stand.

> Hence language is the real medium of human being, if we only see it in the realm that it alone fills out, the realm of human being together, the realm of common understanding of ever replenished common agreement--a realm as indispensable to human life as the air we

breathe. As Aristotle said, man is truly the being who has language. For we should let everything human be spoken to us.[32]

Gadamer's contention that linguistic understanding can be the basis for normative universals or truth claims is subject to the objection that it perpetuates a type of philosophical idealism that a hermeneutical interpretation is intended to avoid. This position has been most forcefully articulated by Richard Rorty who is a leading representative of so-called deconstructivism in current philosophical developments. While Rorty shares Gadamer's emphasis upon hermeneutical interpretation in opposition to the Kantian-Cartesian legacy, he would reject Gadamer's contention that the emphasis upon language can be the basis for hermeneutical ontology. Rorty affirms the radical deconstructivism that he sees to be common to Dewey, Foucault, and Derrida: "that there is nothing deep down inside us except what we have put there ourselves, no criterion that we have not created in the course of creating a practice; no standard of rationality that is not an appeal to such criterion; no rigorous argumentation that is not obedience to our own conventions."[33] There can thus be no alternative way of "grounding" moral commitments, loyalties, or convictions save the fact that the beliefs and desires and emotions that buttress them overlap those of other members of the groups with which we identify for purposes of moral or political deliberation.[34]

In Rorty's view, then, the giving up of a traditional Platonic or an epistemologically centered philosophy does not permit any hope that there can be an alternative foundation in terms of Gadamer's concept of the role of language in human understanding. As Richard Bernstein puts it:

> If Rorty were to comment on Gadamer, he would find all talk of an entirely different notion of truth and knowledge revealed through hermeneutical interpretation to be a form of mystification. Despite Gadamer's incisive critiques of epistemology and the Cartesian legacy, Gadamer is unwittingly a victim of the very Cartesian legacy he is reacting against.[35]

What is objectionable to Rorty's position, however, is his contention that only criteria of normative justification are the social practices or con-

ventions of a particular time and place. It is
difficult to see that Rorty, himself, adheres to this
implication for he displays an obvious commitment to
normative principles that are difficult to reconcile
with his adamant disavowal of any ontological assumptions. This is apparent in his celebration of John
Dewey's pragmatism as an alternative to any type of
"systematic philosophy." Pragmatism, he contends,
rejects the Kantian faith in right concepts of reason,
science, thought, knowledge, or morality that will
shield us against irrationalist resentment and hatred.

> Pragmatism tells us that this hope is vain.
> In this view, the Socratic virtues--willing-
> ness to talk, to listen to other people, to
> weigh consequences of our action upon other
> people--are simply moral virtues.... We are
> not conversing because we have a goal, but
> because a Socratic conversation is an activ-
> ity which is its own end.[36]

But what is the source of Rorty's attachment to
"Socratic virtues"? One can assume his answer is that
it is simply because he happens to be a member of an
American community that affirms such virtues. But
what is the criteria by which I am able to claim that
the virtues of dialogue and conversations within the
particular community to which I am involved has any
intrinsic superiority as against the normative principles of a particular historical community in which
such principles are violated and betrayed? It may be
true there can be no appeal to foundationalist criteria in the sense of a Platonic or Cartesian certitude, but Rorty gives no indication as to what can
be an alternative criteria for the virtues of a
democratic society to which he is obviously
dedicated.

The merit of Gadamer's hermeneutical interpretation is that while he shares Rorty's emphasis upon the
concept of social practice and the virtues of conversation and dialogue, he sees this process as a
creative interplay of interpretation and tradition in
which universal norms can be established. Human
understanding is language bound, but this does not
lead to linguistic relativism. Gadamer subscribes to
the central contention of Aristotle that it is by virtue of the fact man communicates meaning that normative principles of what is right and wrong and what
is harmful and useful is possible. But Gadamer is not
offering the illusory comfort of universal principles

15

that are pregiven or metaphysically grounded. The very idea of a definitive interpretation is intrinsically contradictory. Interpretation is always on the way, pointing to the finitude of human being and human knowing. From the standpoint of theological reflection, for example, the understanding of scripture is never the totality of objective statements but what is addressed to me in a personal way. A text that stirs our interest will not be that it communicates neutral facts to us. We have to get behind such putative facts to awaken our interest in them. We encounter facts in statements that are answers, but a philosophical hermeneutics is more interested in questions than answers. Every statement has to be a response to a question; the only way to understand a statement is to get hold of the question to which the statement is an answer. The affinity of hermeneutics with practical philosophy is confined in that understanding, like action, is never the application of general rules to statements of text to be understood.[37]

Gadamer thus rightly sees Aristotelian praxis as a paradigm for hermeneutical interpretation. For it is an approach to the problem of relating universals to particulars. The ideals of what man ought to be have to be made in concrete situations of human action in which what is required is not technical expertise or scientific knowledge but self-deliberation and prudential wisdom. Gadamer's hermeneutical theory, as an appropriation of Aristotelian praxis, is not to be seen as any conclusive answer to the complex problem of normative reconstruction in face of the decline of confidence in classical foundationalism. But it has been the intent of this essay only to contend that Gadamer's contribution is a constructive move in the direction beyond the dangerous polarizations between objectivism vs. subjectivism, and metaphysical absolutism vs. historical relativism and nihilism.

NOTES

1. Hans Gadamer, Truth and Method (New York: Crossroad Press, 1982), p. 250.

2. Ibid.

3. Ibid., p. 251.

4. Ibid., p. 261.

5. Ibid., p. 264.

6. Ibid., p. 273.

7. Ibid., p. 279.

8. Ibid., p. 280.

9. Ibid., p. 284.

10. Ibid., p. 287.

11. Ibid., p. 289.

12. Ibid., p. 299.

13. Jurgen Habermas, "A Review of Gadamer's Truth and Method," in Understanding and Social Inquiry (Notre Dame: University of Notre Dame Press, 1977), pp. 356-361.

14. Hans Gadamer, Philosophical Hermeneutics, translated and edited by David E. Linge (Berkeley: University of California Press, 1977), p. 33.

15. Ibid., p. 32.

16. Ibid., p. 35.

17. Gadamer, Truth and Method, p. 495.

18. Gadamer, Philosophical Hermeneutics, p. 34.

19. Paul Ricoeur, Hermeneutics and the Human Sciences, edited and translated by John B. Thompson (New York: Cambridge University Press, 1982), p. 99.

20. Ibid., p. 100.

21. Richard Bernstein, Beyond Objectivism and Relativism (Philadelphia: University of Pennsylvania Press, 1983), p. 157.

22. Hans Gadamer, Reason in the Age of Science (Cambridge: MIT Press, 1983), pp. 69-74.

23. Ibid., pp. 83-84.

24. Robert Bellah, The Broken Covenant (New York: Seabury Press, 1975), p. 17.

25. Ibid.

26. Ibid., xiv.

27. Robert Bellah et al., Habits of Heart: Individualism and Commitment in American Life (Berkeley: University of California Press, 1985), chaps. 9-1?

28. Gadamer, Philosophical Hermeneutics, p. 60.

29. Ibid., p. 64.

30. Ibid., p. 65.

31. Ibid., p. 66.

32. Ibid., p. 68.

33. Richard Rorty, Consequences of Pragmatism (Minneapolis: University of Minnesota Press, 1982), p. xlii.

34. Richard Rorty, "Postmodernist Bourgeois Liberalism," Hermeneutics and Praxis (Notre Dame: University of Notre Dame Press, 1985), p. 218.

35. Bernstein, Beyond Objectivism and Relativism, p. 199.

36. Bernstein, Consequences of Pragmatism, p. 172.

37. Gadamer, Reason in the Age of Science, p. 109.

CHAPTER 2

THE HERMENEUTICAL POLITICAL THEORY OF CHARLES TAYLOR: CONTRA RORTY AND FOUCAULT

Charles Taylor is a leading figure in contemporary hermeneutical interpretation along with Hans Gadamer, Jurgen Habermas, Richard Rorty, and Michael Foucault. Among these writers there would be a generally shared opposition to naturalistic, ahistorical features of Enlightenment rationalism, and a common emphasis upon interpretive understanding directed to texts, practices, forms of life, and institutions. But one would find a sharp division between a more radical historicism represented by Rorty and Foucault as opposed to a type of hermeneutical ontology represented by Taylor and Gadamer.

Characteristic of Rorty and Foucault is a thoroughgoing historical relativism in regard to normative evaluation, not only as against a type of classical metaphysics or Platonism but as against reconstructive interpretations that would seek to sustain normative universals within the contingencies of historical, social practice, or (as in the case of Taylor) the attempt to ground the principles of human agency and personhood within a hermeneutical interpretation. In the radical antifoundationalist perspective of Rorty there can be no possibility for normative justification beyond the current practices and conventions of particular historical groups and communities of discourse. What is particularly striking in Foucault's hermeneutical interpretation is a "death of man centered epistemology," which, as Paul Smith points out, constitutes a serious challenge to classical presuppositions of Western humanism. The attack upon foundationalism, he remarks, has been an attack upon some of the major categories of the Western liberal tradition such as freedom, autonomy, dignity, and rights. "It may well be that what is at stake in this seemingly epistemological debate is the very survival of the humanistic tradition of political thought in general and liberal values in particular." Smith poses the question of whether a radical epistemology without a subject can be an intelligible locus for theories of justice and rights. "To what extent can the search for an Archimedean standpoint for knowledge be abandoned and at the same time the pitfalls of relativism, historicism, and ultimately nihilism be avoided?"[1]

It is the thesis of this essay that the hermeneutical theory of Charles Taylor represents a constructive move in the direction of formulating a concept of human agency and personhood that can avoid both the inadequacies of Enlightenment naturalism as well as the radical historical relativism represented by Foucault and Rorty. In defending this thesis it will be the intent to present, first, a general account of Taylor's hermeneutical political theory as a critical reaction to Enlightenment naturalism; second, to stress his defense of humanist concepts of subjective intentionality, freedom, and truth against the deconstructivist analysis of Foucault; and finally, to evaluate Taylor's position in terms of critical dialogue with the positions of both Foucault and Rorty.

I

The concept of human beings as "self-interpreting animals" is a central theme in Taylor's hermeneutical theory, which he views as a thesis about a science of man in opposition to the science of nature that emerged in seventeenth century scientific revolution. The seventeenth century development, he observes, embodies a paradigm of distinction between primary and secondary qualities, the latter as subjective experiences that could not be integrated to a science of the nature of things. Taylor observes that in more recent times this theory of experience has expressed itself in reductionist explanations of human action and experience in terms of physiological and ultimately chemical terms. In this way, it is hoped, we will be able to treat man as an object among objects in terms of properties independent of his experience. The lived experience of sensation, for example, can be treated as "epiphenomena" or a misdescription of what is really a brain state.[2]

Hermeneutical interpretation, in contrast to objectivist analysis, embodies an emphasis upon experiencing emotions as "imports" that are relevant to the desires and purposes of the feeling subject. The experience of shame, for example, is an emotion that a subject experiences in relation to a dimension of his existence as a subject "in whose form of life there figures an aspiration to dignity, to be a presence among men which commands respect."[3] The properties of which this is true are what Taylor calls "subject referring" properties, which can only exist in a world in which there are subjects of experience.

Subject referring properties do not thus fit into an objectivist view of the world because they can only be explicated in experience-dependent terms. On the other hand, they cannot be classed simply as a subjective view of things, for to describe an import is to make a judgment about the way things are which is not simply to be reduced to the way we feel about them. "Beyond the question of whether I feel ashamed is the question whether the situation is really shameful, whether I am rightly or wrongly rationally or irrationally, ashamed."[4] Subject referring emotions, then, have to do with asscribing imports as shame, dignity, pride, feelings of admiration or contempt, moral obligations, and so on. "Our subject referring feelings," he contends, "incorporate a sense of what it is to be human, that is, of what matters to us as human beings."[5] Subject referring properties are central to the meaning of human agency and personhood as the power to evaluate our desires in relationship to qualitative distinctions of higher or lower, virtuous or vicious, more or less fulfilling, more or less noble or base.[6]

Taylor's hermeneutical theory, in terms of political implications, embodies a sharp challenge to the presuppositions of behavioral political science as the endeavor to understand political behavior in terms of "brute data" whose validity is seen to be beyond all interpretive disputes. This would include some acts that could be specified in physical terms as the sending of tanks into the street, seizing people and confining them to cells, and others that can be specified from physical acts by institutional rules such as voting. The behavioral approach would recognize, however, that this would be too narrow, and that it is necessary to consider actions that have meaning for the agent that cannot be exhausted by such descriptions. Behavioral science comes to grips with this by taking the meaning involved in actions as facts about the agent, his beliefs, objective reactions, and values that can be seen as verifiable in the "brute data" sense. This would assume that reactions to the world, events, or symbols can be considered accessible to techniques of opinion surveys and content analysis. While interpretative disputes cannot be verifiable, what can be verified are correlations such as that between assent to propositions and certain behavior, without having to be concerned about how to arbitrate disputes between rival interpretations.[7]

Taylor's objection to behavioral science is that it overlooks the fact that institutional practices

21

cannot be identified in abstraction from the language we use to describe them. The practice of negotiation, for example, allows us to distinguish bargaining in good faith or bad faith or entering into or breaking off negotiations. Inherent in practices of this kind is a certain vision of the agent and his relation to others and to society involving implicit norms such as that of good faith or the norms of rationality and autonomy. These norms have to do with intersubjective meanings that are not just in the minds of actors but in practices that are made up of social relations and mutual actions. Nor can such intersubjective meanings be described in terms of a consensus or convergence of beliefs and can, in fact, be accomplished by cleavage and conflict.[8]

Taylor contends that the intersubjective meanings involved in institutions and practices do not fit the methodological grid of behavioral political inquiry that allows for intersubjective reality only in terms of identifiable brute data. But such practices and institutions that are partly constituted by ways of talking about them are not so identifiable. We have to understand the language, the underlying meaning that constitutes them. This means that we must give up the premise of social reality as brute data. For the meaning underlying practice is open to alternative interpretations, meanings that are subjective and not just causal interactions. It is such common meanings, he argues, that "falls through the net" of behavioral science as an epistemological tradition where knowledge has to be reconstructed from impressions imprinted on the individual subject.[9]

Taylor also challenges the well-entrenched doctrine of behavioral science that values must be separated from facts, prescription from descriptions. Taylor does not deny the value of this distinction insofar as it applies to the nonexistence of logical relations between descriptive predicates and evaluative terms. But Taylor believes that there are two valid points that are overlooked by the so-called non-naturalist view: "1. to apply 'good' may or may not be to commend; but it is always to claim that there are reasons for recommending whatever it is applied to; 2. to say of something that it fulfills a human need, want, or purpose always constitutes prima facie reasons for calling it 'good' and for applying the term, in the absence of overriding considerations."[10]

Taylor's basic objection to the nonnaturalist view is that it overlooks the legitimacy of reasons for moral judgment in relation to what men desire, need, or seek as opposed to simply the expression of irrational dislikes, fears, and so on. Taylor gives an illustration of this in disagreement over the statement that "to make medical care available to more people is 'good.'" A denial of this might be that the world population would grow too fast; there are more urgent claims on scarce resources, and so forth. Such opposition would be at least intelligible in contrast to a view: "there would be too many doctors" or "there would be too many people dressed in white," which can be viewed as expression of a dislike rather than an intelligible argument. What Taylor is arguing, then, is that a claim to say of something that it fulfill a human need, want, or purpose is at least a prima facie reason for calling it good.

> It is, thus, valid to contend that what is conducive to human happiness is adequate grounds. This does not mean that all argument is foreclosed. We can try to show that men degenerate in various ways if they seek only happiness and that certain things which also make men unhappy are necessary for their development. Or we can try to show that there is a higher and lower happiness, that most men seek under this title only pleasure, and that this turns them away from genuine fulfillment; and so on. But unless we can bring up some countervailing consideration, we cannot deny a thesis of this kind. The fact that we can always bring up such countervailing considerations means that we can never say that "good" means conducive to human happiness. But that something is conducive to human happiness, or in general to the fulfillment of human needs, purposes, and wants, is a prima facie reason for calling it good, which stands unless countered.[11]

In considering Taylor's opposition to so-called nonnaturalist positions, it would be important to avoid a possible confusion. Taylor is clearly opposed to a narrow naturalistic reductionism that would equate normative principles with simply the fulfillment of desires or the "pains and pleasures" calculus of utilitarianism. But he is strongly affirmative of a classical Aristotelian view that normative principles are rooted in human nature in a broader sense of what has intrinsic worth and value beyond simply the fulfillment of desires.[12]

It is this perspective that is also the basis of
Taylor's opposition to the atomism that he sees to be
a product of the seventeenth century contract theory
and the primacy of rights doctrines associated with
John Locke and contemporary exponents of this position
such as Robert Nozick. Taylor defends a social view
of man as one that holds that an essential constitutive condition of seeking the human good is bound up
with being in society. Man cannot be a candidate for
the realization of the human good outside of a community of language and mutual discourse about the good
and bad, just and unjust. The basic error of atomism,
he contends, is that it fails to take account of the
degree to which the free individual with his own goals
and aspirations is himself only possible within a certain kind of civilization having to do with the rule
of law, rules of equal respect, habits of common deliberation, of common association and cultural
self-development.[13]

While Taylor shows an obvious affinity to the
Aristotelian concept of community, it should be emphasized that he is not adhering to the traditional Greek
view of man as a rational animal but rather to a
twentieth century shift towards the centrality of
language in regard to human meaning. But he stresses
that this is not a radical shift if we recognize that
the Aristotelian concept of logos incorporates a sense
of the relationship of speech and thought. There has
been a shift, but it is one within the complex
"thought/language," the displacement of the center of
gravity. Basic to this transition, he contends, is an
emphasis on an expressive as opposed to a designative
concept of meaning. Characteristic of designative
meaning is a theory of language that fits into the
objectifying character of modern natural science, the
view that the meaning of sentences has to do with a
state of affairs in the world. But expressive meaning
has to do with subject-related properties, a view of
language as a certain mode of "being in the world"
that is not just reflective but by which we come to
have human emotions and feelings such as indignation,
condemnation of the unjust, admiration of remarkable
traits, and so on.[14]

Language, Taylor contends, serves a threefold
function in bringing to awareness what was formerly
only implicit; putting things into public space of
intersubjective communication; and the medium through
which some of our most important concerns impinge upon
all of us. Language, thus, has a "constitutive"

dimension. It does not only serve to describe or represent things; certain phenomena central to human life are partly constituted by language. The language we use enters into an essential part of human feelings, goals, and social relationships and practices. It is not only feelings but also the actual social structure of our relations with others that are partly defined by language: forms of hierarchy, modes of equality, intimacy, and distance. This is not to say such relations are not shaped by power and property but that power and property are, themselves, shaped by language. These relationships require a degree of common understanding by participants illustrated in the types of political regimes that have come down to us from the Greek polis and the Roman republic where there was recognition that a concept of equality was impossible without some formulation of a demand for equality, where equality was bound up with norms of who should rule and how.[15]

II

While Taylor views hermeneutical interpretation in opposition to Enlightenment naturalism, he is equally critical of the radical historicism represented by Michael Foucault. Taylor would be able to acknowledge a commonality with Foucault as a general rejection of a correspondence theory of knowledge and as an emphasis upon the centrality of language, text, and social practice in regard to human understanding and knowledge. Foucault's contribution to hermeneutical interpretation centers upon his theory of discourse: the contention that discourse is a regulative social practice and, hence, partakes of power as well as knowledge--the fusion of power and knowledge in the practices that comprise history. In his study of medical practices, human sciences, criminal punishment, and mental illness, Foucault has provided an effective illumination of how particular discursive formations define components of power and how theory shapes practices in Western history.[16]

But the place where Foucault's hermeneutical interpretation clashes with that of Taylor is its thoroughgoing antihumanism: the rejection of those theories that give to the human subject a central place in human knowledge and action and his posture of "Nietzschean neutrality" in regard to normative implications of changing social practices inspired by the eighteenth century Enlightenment.[17] Here it should be emphasized that while Taylor makes a strong attack

upon the presuppositions of Enlightenment naturalism
(as previously noted), his concepts of man as a self-
interpreting animal and human agency bears a strong
affinity with a facet of Enlightenment thought represented by Kant, and it would also be important to
emphasize that Taylor is strongly committed to the
broadly humanist concerns and aspirations of the
Enlightenment heritage. It is thus understandable
that Taylor finds Foucault's analysis
"disconcerting."[18] Taylor comments that Foucault
seems to offer an analysis of what has happened and
what we have become and, in fact, some notion of a good
unrealized or repressed in history that we thereby
understand better how to rescue. But what Taylor
finds disconcerting is Foucault's repudiation of this
suggestion. While he seems to bring evils to light,
he wants to distance himself from what would seem to
follow that the negation of these evils promotes a
good. For Foucault the ideal of a liberating truth
is a profound illusion; there is no truth that can be
espoused, defended, or rescued against systems of
power. "We can only step from one to another."[19]

Taylor acknowledges that Foucault's studies on
criminal punishment provide us a dramatic insight into
the cruelty and sadism of the execution of Damiens as
an illustration of the meaning of punishment within a
medieval cosmi-political order of things. What
Foucault seems to be providing us is the obverse side
of a modern identity where a new notion of good has
arisen: a modern humanitarianism that since the
eighteenth century has been associated with concepts
of the preservation of life, the fulfillment of human
needs, the relief from human suffering. It is this
development that disposes us to envisage a change in
philosophies of punishment that is at least a gain, and
a critique of the older mystification in the name of
which human beings were sacrificed and where terrible
suffering was inflicted. But Foucault does not take
this stance. In contrast to classical concepts of
sovereignty/obedience, we have a new system of dominance and subjugation. Since the eighteenth century
the new social sciences, the new disciplines in
armies, schools, and hospitals are formations of new
modes of domination. The new philosophy of punishment, for example, is not inspired by humanitarianism
but by the need to control: "people are measured,
classified, and made better subjects to a control
which tends to normalization."[20]

What Taylor finds disconcerting about Foucault's
analysis is the "Nietzschean derived neutrality"[21]

between different systems of power that prevents any evaluation that would seem to arise from his analysis. What one ought to expect, in other words, is that if forms of power are the repression of an authentic dimension of human nature, then we should be able to speak of a liberation that is helped by the unmasking of falsehood, a liberation aided by truth. But Foucault's Nietzschean neutrality refuses this.

Another line of critique that Taylor believes one can take up against Foucault is his one-sidedness. Taylor acknowledges that Foucault provides a great deal of insight and originality in bringing neglected areas to light. The disciplines that helped to found modern society based on contract and responsible government, Taylor would concede, are now often serving bureaucratic modes of irresponsible power that are sapping democracy. But Taylor's objection to Foucault's analysis is that it is an over-simplification. His opposition of the old model of power based on sovereignty/obedience and the new one based on dominance/subjugation leaves out everything in Western history animated by civic humanism and ana-logous movements. "And this means a massive amount of what is specific in our civilization."[22]

But Taylor's more basic critique of Foucault's analysis is that it embodies an ultimate incoherence in regard to several key dimensions. One is the concept of "power without a subject."[23] Taylor would not deny the value of Foucault's analysis in setting aside the old model of power as one person or class exercising sovereign control over another. He would concede Foucault's insight that we have to deal with combinations, alignments--the mutual effects of oppo-sition; his contention that the macro context of state or ruling class forms a context in which microrela-tions come to be modified, the endless relation and reciprocal conditions between global and micro con-texts. What Taylor objects to, however, is Foucault's contention that the context of relations of power involves a strategic logic that cannot be attributed to any conscious purpose. In Taylor's view it is possible to attribute purposefulness without purpose to history, a logic to events without design. An example would be a political terrorism in response to self-hatred and a response to a sense of emptiness that would be a better explanation than its avowed goals. It is a mistake, he would concede, to think that any intelligible relation between a pattern and our purpose is one where a pattern is consciously willed, but it is his contention that all patterns have to be made intelligible in relation to conscious action.

Taylor does not deny that power must be understood in a context and that technology and control cannot be explained simply in terms of the actions of a single person or class. But you do need to explain it in relation to the purposefulness of a human action in which it arises and which it has come to shape. To give absolute priority to the structure makes exactly as little sense as the equal and opposite error of subjectivism.

The second incoherence Taylor sees in Foucault's analysis is his concept of "power without freedom, or truth."[24] In the view of Taylor "power belongs to the semantic field from which truth and freedom cannot be excluded; it cannot be separated from the nature of some relative lifting of this restraint from the unimpeded fulfillment of these desires and purposes."[25] Power does not make sense without at least the idea of liberation, and mask or falsehood makes no sense without a corresponding notion of truth. Foucault's thesis, he contends, is a relativist perspective that does not allow for liberation through transformation of power relations. What Foucault leaves out is the possibility of a change of life forms that can be understood as a move towards a greater acceptance of truth and, under certain conditions, a greater freedom. Taylor believes that we have become certain things in Western civilization; our humanitarianism has helped to define a political identity we share, rooted in our more basic infrapolitical understanding of what it is to be a person. These concepts, to be sure, are the subject of perpetual revision and conflict, and we dispute among ourselves as to comparative weightings and evaluations. "But we cannot shrug them off," Taylor contends. "They define humanity, politics for us. This means that we can look at the kind of change Foucault described, from seventeenth century punishments to our own, in a way which renders them partly commensurable. It is not for nothing that we are the descendants and heirs of the people who so tortured Damiens." But our present respect for the dignity of life, Taylor points out, was already there in that Christian civilization. What made them act so differently was the sense of belonging to a cosmic order that is different from ours. "But this difference cannot be seen in a purely relativist light."[26] For there has been an advance in our understanding of the world that represents a significant gain of truth.

This is not to deny the losses, which, indeed, Foucault has well documented, the forms of dehumanization that have been the product of an instrumental reason. This is why there is such a malaise in our civilization. "The reality of history is mixed and messy." Foucault's monolithic relativism, Taylor contends, is plausible only if we take a detached outsider perspective. "But we have a history and identity in which we have become something. Questions of truth and freedom can rise for us in transformations we undergo or project."[27]

Taylor believes that parts of Foucault's writings, in fact, indicate that he does believe that Western civilization made a false turn with the Christian preoccupation with purity and self-renunciation and that we need to return to ancient concept of good life as a self making, an "aesthetic of existence"[28] that would make one's life a work of art. It would thus be understandable that Foucault wants to distance himself from the banners of truth and freedom that have betrayed that heritage.

Taylor wonders if Foucault, before his death, was moving towards recovery of the source that has been lost. At this point, Taylor concludes, the debate begins on issues that Foucault's mode of expression obscures.

> 1. Can we really step outside the identity we have developed in Western civilization to such a degree that we can repudiate all that comes to us from the Christian understanding of the will? Can we toss aside the whole tradition of Augustinian inwardness?
> 2. Granted we really can set this aside, is the resulting aesthetic of existence all that admirable? These questions are hard to separate, and even harder to answer. But they are among the most fundamental raised by the admirable work of Michael Foucault.[29]

III

In defending Taylor's hermeneutical political theory it is necessary to consider both a rebuttal to Taylor's criticism of Foucault and also the reinforcement of Foucault's position provided in the position of Richard Rorty. In a defense of Foucault against Taylor, William Connally's principle reproach to Taylor is that he does not show that his ontological position is any more viable. Given that Taylor himself rejects a correspondence theory of knowledge and that he affirms a hermeneutical principle of human understanding, is not Taylor's opposition to Foucault a residual commitment to a teleological philosophy that Foucault's analysis is designed to discredit? If so, Connally asks, how can Taylor's position be sustained in the modern age?[30]

It is essentially the same kind of reproach to Taylor that Richard Rorty would make. In a debate in the Review of Metaphysics, Rorty contends that Taylor's distinction between subject-related vs. non-subject-related terms and his distinction between human vs. natural science can no longer be made. In making such distinctions, Rorty contends, Taylor is clinging to a Cartesian-Kantian legacy that he supposedly disavows.[31] Rorty, as much as Foucault, believes that it is impossible to step outside our skins, linguistic and other, within which we do our thinking and self-criticism. What ties Dewey and Foucault, James and Nietzsche together, he believes, is the sense that there is nothing deep down inside us except what we have put there ourselves, no criterion not created in the course of creating a practice, no standard of rationality that is not an appeal to such criteria, no rigorous argument that is not an obedience to our conventions. But Rorty would deny that his position amounts to a philosophical relativism or nihilism. Rorty proffers what he calls an "edifying philosophy" as opposed to systematic philosophy as the effort to keep conversation going rather than the discovery of truth. The danger that edifying discourse seeks to avert is that some given vocabulary or discourse would be the norm. The resulting freezing over of civilization would lead to the dehumanization of human beings. "To keep conversations going is a sufficient aim of philosophy."[32]

Seeking to make a defense of Taylor's hermeneutical theory against the positions of Foucault and Rorty centers upon the problem of the role of the subject in historical action and normative evaluation. The merit of Taylor's critique of Foucault's concept of "power without a subject" is that it avoids a doctrinaire or dogmatic formulation on this issue. Taylor's protest against Foucault, it was seen, is against the extreme "death of man" epistemology of his discursive analysis. Taylor recognizes that it is a mistake to think that the only intelligible reality between a pattern and our conscious purpose is a direct one where the pattern is consciously willed: a hangup, he agrees, that comes down to us from a classical Cartesian-empiricist view of the mind. His point is not that all patterns issue from conscious activity but that all patterns have to be made intelligible in relation to conscious action. Taylor takes a balanced view that there not only can but there must be something between total subjectivity on the one hand and the absolute priority of the structural background that Foucault leaves us.

Foucault's analysis, as Paul Smith points out, is part of a larger reaction to the concept of the primacy of the subject in the modern era that has led to an oversocialized concept of man in which we are so completely determined by the place and function we occupy, there is nothing left over.

> The idea we are molded by circumstances and institutions has ceased to be controversial. But to say that everything we do can be explained by places and functions is by no means obvious. Individuals are never merely representatives of a set of prescribed roles, nor can human actions be explained solely in causal or functional terms. Social actors must be understood at least in part as intentional subjects acting in response to an understood situation and whose actions must also be seen in terms of symbolic or meaningful character for the agents themselves.

Smith rightly stresses that the proclamation of the death of man in Foucault is not simply a prophecy of doom; it does not mean the human species will disappear. "What will disappear, he fears, is not man, as such, but one historically specific conception of man as a thinking and active subject who is simultaneously both knower and maker of the world. What will also disappear is the attempt to ground the human in terms of purportedly permanent attributes like freedom, autonomy, dignity, or rights."[33]

It is difficult to see that the positions of Foucault and Rorty can escape charges of relativist-nihilist implications with which they have been frequently charged. This would be particularly true of Foucault who, as Taylor convincingly argues, adopts a

Nietzschean stance that neutralizes evaluations that arise out of his analysis and refuses to allow for any liberation through transformation of power relations. In a critique of Foucault, Stephen White makes essentially the same point: "He provides us ultimately with no way of distinguishing the resistance of the Women's Movement or the Polish Solidarity Movement from say the Ku Klux Klan or Jim Jones' Peoples Temple. Of course, Foucault himself would never have endorsed such things. But this is not the point; the point is his denials have an ad hoc quality."[34]

Rorty is perhaps less vulnerable to the charge of nihilist implications in the sense that while he rejects the possibility of objective truth, he argues for the virtues of open dialogue and conversation that he sees as the best safeguard against the dehumanization of man in a closed society. It would thus not be fair to accuse Rorty of the Nietzschean stance of neutrality that Taylor associates with Foucault. The problem in Rorty's position, however, is that he sees no basis for justification for the humanist values he obviously subscribes to beyond the fact of his membership in a particular historical community that happens to uphold such values. This is significantly revealed in his response to the charge of nihilism that is made against his position. This is the charge that since he sees normative judgments rooted in the consensus of a specific community, then how is he able to recognize the human dignity of someone who is not a part of a shared community: "a child found wandering in the woods, a remnant of a slaughtered nation whose temples have been razed and whose books have been burned, has no share in human dignity."

Rorty's response is that it is part of the tradition of our community that the stranger from whom all dignity has been stripped is to be taken in, to be "reclothed with dignity. This Jewish and Christian element in our tradition, he acknowledges, is "gratefully invoked by freedom loving atheists" like himself.[35] But surely Rorty is aware of the fact that the force of the Christian-Judaic position is that one must honor the principle of human dignity not simply because it happens to be the conventional practice of the particular community in which I am involved, but because it has a universal validity. The fact that Rorty confesses that he is "grateful" for being a member of a civilization that respects human dignity would seem to indicate that he does have reasons for the justification of this principle in opposition to historical practices that have violated it either in other communities or in his own community during certain historical periods. Yet, the terms of Rorty's deconstructivist epistemology do not permit the establishment of criteria by which there can be any adjudication between rival historical practices and conventions. The difficulty of Rorty's position, as Richard Bernstein points out, is that he gives us no criteria for discriminating between the better and the worse. This cannot be a matter of arbitrary endorsing of one set of values over competing values but rather trying to give stronger historical reasons to support one side or the other.[36]

Charles Guignon makes a similar critique: "Rorty sings the praises of current language games drifting around in the current public world." In the view of Guignon, Rorty is adopting a version of pragmatism in which nothing could count as justification for one way of speaking over another. "This seems to imply that for Rorty's pragmatism what seems right is right. There is no way to think about purposes and goals outside of whatever vocabularies are in play, with the result that we can only think about means to ends and their cost of attainment within our current vocabularies with their built-in ends."[37]

It is here that Taylor's hermeneutical theory provides a corrective to historical relativism of Rorty's position; for intrinsic to Taylor's hermeneutical interpretation, it has been seen, is the emphasis upon subject referring emotions having to do with our sense of shame, pride, moral obligations that open us to a sense of what it is to be human. And what it means to be fully human, Taylor believes, requires a certain type of society. A man cannot be a moral subject and candidate for realization of human good outside a community and language of mutual discourse about good and bad, just and unjust, a recognition that the free individual is possible only in a civilization embodying practices of the rule of law, habits of common deliberation, cultural self-development without which the individual would atrophy.

In his emphasis upon the virtues of free and open conversation, Rorty is quite obviously affirming this type of institutional structure, but his insistence upon the relativism of competing language games provides no basis for how such an institutional structure can be given any intrinsic justification beyond saying that "this is the way we do things" within the particular communities with which we are identified.[38]

33

The inadequacies of Foucault-Rorty positions do not, of course, establish that Taylor's hermeneutical theory can be easily defended against the charge that (despite his disavowals) he is still clinging to a Kantian-Cartesian ontology or to a type of philosophical teleology that is no longer credible in the modern age. It has not been the intent of this essay to adjudicate this issue but only to contend that Taylor is among hopeful possibilities (along with similar efforts by such writers as Gadamer, Ricoeur, Habermas) for a constructive movement beyond the despair to which the deconstructivist positions of Foucault and Rorty must inevitably lead.

In response to Connally's defense of Foucault, Taylor makes his own best defense on this point. If we want to go on living, he contends, we have to proffer some schematic of self-interpretation and not just denounce the ones around us. Taylor would not deny that some of our most inspiring self-interpretations have been guilty of obvious ambiguities; the fact, for example, that the Greek polis was based on slavery and the exclusion of women and that the modern demand for universal suffrage was for manhood suffrage. But this ought not to foreclose the issue of truth and liberation and that some gains are possible.

Taylor argues that despite the inadequacies of a correspondence theory of truth, we still need a concept of self-interpretation as constitutive and, as such, a recognition of what is in varying degrees distortive or authentic, a possibility that Foucault seems to close out. As to the contention that he is clinging to a type of philosophical teleology, Taylor's response is that if this means a Hegelian view of a design in history, that is not what he intends. But if by teleology one means a distinction between what is authentic vs. what is distortive, then he confesses that is what he does mean. How is this to be defended? Taylor does not profess to have a definitive answer, but he is surely justified in contending that what he does seek to proffer is at least not anachronistic, that it is no worse than its rivals and certainly better than a Nietzschean view of truth as imposition.[39]

1. Stephen Smith, "Althusser's Marxism Without a Knowing Subject," American Political Science Review, September 1985, p. 642.

2. Charles Taylor, Human Agency and Language: Philosophical Papers, vol. 1 (Cambridge: Cambridge University Press, 1985), p. 47.

3. Ibid., p. 53.

4. Ibid., p. 55.

5. Ibid., p. 60.

6. Ibid., p. 61.

7. Charles Taylor, Philosophy and the Human Sciences: Philosophical Papers, vol. 2 (Cambridge: Cambridge University Press, 1985), p. 29.

8. Ibid., p. 36.

9. Ibid., p. 44.

10. Ibid., p. 82.

11. Ibid., p. 89.

12. Ibid., pp. 266-270.

13. Ibid., p. 309.

14. Taylor, Human Agency and Language: Philosophical Papers, vol. 1, p. 234.

15. Ibid., p. 272.

16. Foucault's best-known works in translation include The Order of Things (New York: Random House, 1973); Madness and Civilization (New York: Mentor Books, 1965); The Birth of the Clinic (New York: Random House, 1973); The History of Sexuality (New York: Random House, 1980).

17. See Foucault, The Order of Things, pp. 340-343, 385-387. For critical discussion of this feature of Foucault's analysis see Mark Cousins and

Athar Hussain, <u>Michael Foucault</u> (New York: St. Martins Press, 1984), pp. 262-266; J. G. Merquior, <u>Foucault</u> (Berkeley: University of California Press, 1985), chap. 4.

18. Taylor, <u>Philosophy and the Human Sciences</u>: <u>Philosophical Papers</u>, vol. 2, p. 152.

19. Ibid., p. 20.

20. Ibid., p. 158.

21. Ibid., p. 163.

22. Ibid., p. 166.

23. Ibid., p. 167.

24. Ibid., p. 174.

25. Ibid., p. 176.

26. Ibid., p. 181.

27. Ibid., p. 182.

28. Ibid., p. 183.

29. Ibid., p. 184.

30. William Connally, "Taylor, Foucault and Otherness," <u>Political Theory</u>, August 1985, p. 373.

31. Richard Rorty, "A Reply to Dreyfus and Taylor," <u>Review of Metaphysics</u>, September 1980, pp. 39-46.

32. Richard Rorty, <u>Philosophy and the Mirror of Nature</u> (Princeton: Princeton University Press, 1979), p. 378

33. Smith, p. 652.

34. Stephen White, "Foucault's Challenge to Critical Theory," <u>American Political Science Review</u>, June 1966, p. 430.

35. Richard Rorty, "Postmodernist Bourgeois Liberalism,"in <u>Hermeneutics and Praxis</u>, edited by Robert Hollinger (Notre Dame: University of Notre Dame Press, 1985), pp. 219-220.

36. Richard Bernstein, <u>Beyond Objectivism and Relativism</u> (Philadelphia: University of Pennsylvania Press, 1983), p. 8.

37. Charles Guignon, "Saving Heidegger from Rorty," <u>Philosophy and Phenomenological Research</u>, March 1986, p. 409.

38. Rorty, "Postmodernist Bourgeois Liberalism," p. 318.

39. Charles Taylor, "Connally, Foucault and Truth," <u>Political Theory</u>, August 1985, p. 385.

CHAPTER 3

MICHAEL POLANYI: THE MORAL IMPERATIVES
OF A FREE SOCIETY

The hermeneutical interpretations of Gadamer and
Taylor, as considered in the previous chapters, are
characterized by an emphasis upon historical
consciousness that presupposes a distinction between
the human and natural sciences. What is distinctive
in the writings of Polanyi is a development in the
philosophy of science that rejects the objectivist
criteria of scientific positivism, emphasizing a hermeneutical dimension of human understanding that would
seek to overcome the disjunction between scientific
and humanistic inquiry. While Polanyi's theory of
personal knowledge has been most commonly discussed in
the framework of issues pertaining to the philosophy
of science, his writings embody significant ethical-
political implications related to the issues of
freedom and liberation that are central to the concerns of other exponents of hermeneutical interpretations that are the focus of this study. It is the
intent of this chapter to emphasize Polanyi's contribution to the problem of defining the normative ideals
of democracy in an age characterized by the erosion of
both the metaphysical certitudes of classical political philosophy as well as interpretations that stem
from the heritage of scientific rationalism.

An appreciation of Polanyi's contribution requires
a brief examination of this problem as it stems from
implications inherent in the theory of knowledge
underlying the intellectual premises of Western
liberalism. John Locke's theory of knowledge constituted a vigorous attack upon the existence of innate
ideas. All ideas, in the view of Locke, come from
experience: the objects of sensation are one source
of ideas we have of sensible qualities as white and
yellow, heat and cold. The operation of our minds is
the other source of ideas, as in thinking, doubting,
reasoning--what the mind gets by reflection on its own
operations within itself. It was David Hume who
showed that by adhering strictly to an empirical
theory of knowledge, as formulated by Locke, skepticism is the necessary result. If the mind can know
nothing outside itself, no comparison of ideas can
prove a matter of fact. The theory of cause and
effect has no empirical basis; all that one can say is

that one event proceeds or follows another. But once we label one the cause and the other the effect, we are indulging in metaphysical speculation without adequate empirical basis.

The central importance of Hume's critique in terms of implications for political philosophy was what it embodied as a challenge to the concept of a "law of nature" that Locke believed to be the basis for the claim to natural rights of life, liberty, and property. In terms of Hume's critique Locke's theory of knowledge was not consistent with his political philosophy; a supposed "law of nature" as the basis for the claims of individual natural rights was no more capable of verification than laws of cause and effect governing the behavior of physical phenomena. The consequence of Hume's critique was a radical skepticism towards the belief that reason can provide an objective basis for moral principles. Reason can tell us how to achieve a desirable end but it cannot tell us if the end is good or bad; reason is and ought to be the slave of passions and can never pretend to any other office than to serve and obey them.

It was Hume's conclusion that the only basis for morality resides in the self-interest that motivates men to submit to the convenience of mutually advantageous rules and an instinctive capacity for sympathy or benevolent tendencies that makes society possible. Such feelings, he believed, give pleasure to ourselves as well as others, and hence there is no conflict between selfish and social sentiments. But in no sense does Hume see these tendencies as the basis for universal moral standards; they are but conventions of society that can be explained by history or anthropology, but they cannot claim validity in any but a relative sense of being generally convenient and in accordance with man's estimate of utility.

In light of Hume's critique, the problem of defining the normative ideals of democracy moved in two possible directions. One is an implication made fashionable by contemporary logical positivism that involves the contention that moral judgments are nothing but the subjective preferences of individuals that can claim no universal or objectiv validity. Such a position has its defenders as an approach to defining the moral foundation of democracy on grounds that it implies a commitment to tolerance and the principle of free inquiry against any type of philosophical absolutism. But the obvious objection to logical positivism is that if no values can be asserted as having any universal or objective validity, then there is no reason why freedom, itself, should be regarded as an exception.

A second tendency follows from Hume's contention that the only basis for morality resides in the self-interest that motivates man to mutually advantageous rules, an implication formalized in nineteenth century utilitarianism. This embodied a departure from Hume's skepticism, however, in the confidence that moral guidelines could be established as a scientific calculus of pains and pleasures and that democracy could be thus founded upon the principle of "the greatest happiness of the greatest number." The obvious weakness of utilitarianism is both the fact it involves a common version of the "naturalistic fallacy" that moral imperatives can be deductions from natural inclinations and desires, as well as the fact that it lends itself to an ideological support for the unbridled pursuit of individual egoism and self-interest.

The difficulties of defining the normative ideals of democracy in terms of philosophical implications that follow from the radical skepticism of Hume serves to explain the powerful attraction of Kant's ethical theory as the effort to overcome the impasse left by Hume's critique. The central achievement of Kant stems from a radical bifurcation of the universe between a scientific world of empirical laws and effects (phenomena) vs. a world as it really is (noumena) that is accessible only through the moral will. As creatures of desire, our actions belong to the world of empirical cause and effect and are completely determined. But Kant believed that there is a moral or "transcendental self," which is free and able to transcend the phenomenal world and bring us into contact with the real or noumenal world in which man becomes conscious of moral obligation and the conflict between what is and what ought to be. It is in the consciousness of moral obligation that we experience our freedom as a recognition that the moral law is not something imposed from without but from within. Moral behavior is action in conformity to the idea of law, in doing what reason prescribes as our duty as opposed to personal advantage or self-interest. But Kantian theory, it is widely recognized, perpetuates a central deficiency of Enlightenment rationalism: a radical dualism of mind and body that comes from Descartes through Hume. This springs from his central contention that moral universals are the product of what is given to the practical reason of an autonomous will in opposition to deterministic laws of cause and effect that govern the world of nature as understood by the theoretical reason of scientific inquiry.

The fundamental inadequacy of Kantian perspective, as Majorie Green points out, is the Cartesian image of a thinking mind over a dead nature, making impossible the understanding of man as historical, rooted in the world of living organisms.[1] The conclusions of Kant were inevitable so long as the Newtonian concept of the nature of scientific inquiry was unquestioned. Polanyi represents an influential development in the philosophy of science that challenges the Newtonian model, providing a basis for overcoming the Kantian dualism in which the moral imperatives of practical reason become divorced from the theoretical reason of scientific understanding.

Polanyi's theory of personal knowing can at the same time be seen as a continuity with a Kantian implication (to be more fully discussed in the final chapter on Ricoeur) that the personal quest for truth appears at the horizon of my intended goals as an "ontological hope," truth as a "regulative idea" in the task of a unifying knowledge from the side of the subject, a truth that stretches between the poles of my personal situation and what I aspire to as something universal. The essence of this Kantian concept, it will be seen, is correspondent to Polanyi's conviction that while the truth claim of the scientist embodies a personal dimension beyond an objectivist criteria of verification, this claim is not simply a subjective state of mind but a conviction held with a <u>universal intent</u>. It is this aspect of Polanyi's contribution, from the standpoint of the philosophy of science, that converges with the hermeneutical ontologies of Gadamer and Taylor as a movement in a direction beyond objectivism vs. historical relativism; beyond the dualism of subjective vs. objective, fact vs. value, reason vs. faith fostered by the tradition of scientific positivism, and his conviction that the values of a democratic society (civil liberties, free inquiry, the pursuit of truth and justice) constitute the premises of all forms of personal knowing both scientific and humanistic.

It is the thesis of this essay that Polanyi makes an important contribution to the problem of defining the ethical foundations of democracy in terms that would avoid the inadequacies of classical metaphysics as well as the philosophical implications of Enlightenment rationalism. But Polanyi's political philosophy is also characterized by a serious difficulty. This appears in a paradoxical implication: on the one hand a powerful critique of what he sees to be the nihilist implications of Enlightenment rationalism and its association with the emergence of totalitarian ideologies; on the other hand, his equally strong affirmation of what has been a central product of Enlightenment rationalism: the autonomous, self-regulating mechanism of the market economy. What is lacking in Polanyi's analysis, at this point, is a recognition that the spiritual foundations of a free society, which he acknowledges, requires a commitment to the concept of a common good that stands not only in opposition to the dangers of totalitarian statism, but also to the radical individualism of the market economy.

I

Polanyi believes that the philosophical premises of liberalism and the Enlightenment, although animated by a passion for liberation from religious dogmatism and authority, have actually contributed to the destruction of the meaning of freedom. Anglo-American liberalism, as formulated by Milton and Locke, was a protest against the authority of Aristotle and the demand for freedom of thought as the best means for approximation to truth in a "free and open battle of wits."[2] Closely related to this was a concept of philosophical doubt as argued by Locke: since there can be no certainty in matters of religion, then there can be no warrant for imposition of views on others. The doctrines of free thought--antiauthoritarianism and philosophical doubt--reached its ascendency in the philosophy of the Enlightenment, in the radical skepticism of Voltaire and the French Encyclopedists.

The mood of the French Enlightenment was one of supreme confidence in the possibility of peace and freedom and the relief of mankind from all social ills. But the twentieth century was the realization of the false expectations raised by the Enlightenment: the emergence of nihilism and totalitarianism. Polanyi believes that this is where the inconsistency of a liberalism based on philosophical doubt becomes apparent: "freedom of thought is destroyed by the extension of doubt to the field of traditional ideals, which includes the basis for freedom of thought."[3]

The only reason that this destructive process did not occur in Anglo-American experience, Polanyi contends, was due to the fact of a speculative restraint that meant that traditional ethical standards were not actually supplanted in practice. The utilitarian calculus of pleasure and pain started by Locke, for example, was given lip service, but traditional ethical standards were not actually replaced by new purposes. Thus the moral aspirations of the age of reason--the desire for justice, the detestation of social evils--could continue to sway public opinion despite the fact that these moral forces had no true justification in the utilitarian, materialist philosophies of the age. The speculative and practical restraints that saved liberalism, Polanyi believes, were due to the religious character of liberalism and the fact that democratic institutions were securely established when religious beliefs were still strong. But Polanyi believes that these protective restraints were absent in those parts of Europe based on the French Enlightenment, which was antireligious, and where there were no restraints on skeptical speculation or standards of morality embodied in democratic institutions. This gave birth to substitutes for universal standards of human behavior: the romantic cult of unrestrained nationalism, the Hegelian enthronement of reason immanent in history; the Marxist view of history as the product of class conflict arising from the mode of production.

Revolutions of the twentieth century, Polanyi contends, show how the philosophies that guided these revolutions were originally justified by antiauthoritarian and skeptical formulas of liberty. But this had the consequence of setting men free even from obligations toward truth and justice where reason becomes the rationalization of predetermined desires held or secured by force alone. Polanyi believes that freedom of thought is rendered pointless and must disappear where reason and morality are deprived of their status as a force in their own right.

When a judge in a court of law can no longer appeal to law and justice; when neither a witness, nor the newspapers nor even a scientist reporting on his experiment can speak the truth as he knows it, when in public life there is no moral principle commanding respect; when the revelations of religion and art are denied any substance; then there are no grounds left in which any individual can

43

fully make a stand against the rulers of the day, such is the logic of totalitarianism.[4]

Polanyi's contention that twentieth century totalitarianism can be seen as consequence of the philosophical doubt and skepticism engendered by liberalism and the Enlightenment must, of course, be considered controversial. One obvious objection to this contention is simply that it involves an exaggerated view of the role of ideas and moral passions in influencing political movements, and that Polanyi fails to recognize the complexity of socioeconomic, historical conditions that must be assessed in explaining the rise of totalitarianism.

But whatever degree of importance one may give to the role of ideas and philosophical tendencies, it would be difficult to establish any direct connection between totalitarian ideologies and the intellectual climate fostered by liberalism. Fascist ideology was an eclectic combination of ideas drawn from the racist theories of Gobineau, romantic nationalism, social Darwinism, Hegel's concept of the absolute state, Nietzsche's doctrine of the "will to power." Fascism, as such, was an explicit attack upon liberal ideals of equality, humanitarianism, and parliamentary democracy. Polanyi's answer to this, as noted above, is that liberalism, as a form of philosophical doubt and skepticism, created an intellectual climate that was hospitable to the emergence of Fascism. The moral idealism associated with liberalism was sustained in Anglo-American experience only because of a legacy of traditional religious authority and institutional structures of democracy that prevented the actual implementation of the philosophical premises of liberalism. The absence of such restraints on continental Europe, he contends, made liberalism susceptible to the appeal of nihilist ideologies.

The problem with this contention is that it amounts to little more than a rather strained hypothesis that what was outwardly an obvious antagonism between liberalism and totalitarianism was actually founded upon an intellectual affinity. A further objection to Polanyi's characterization of twentieth century totalitarianism is the absence of any acknowledgment of differences between Fascism and Marxism. It is plausible enough to argue that both Fascism and Stalinist-communism embody similar manifestations of a totalitarian nihilism. But this overlooks a long tradition of a humanist, anti-Soviet

44

Marxism that is in clear antagonism to Fascist principles and ideals.

What remains valid in Polanyi's analysis, however, is that the intellectual climate engendered by liberalism and the Enlightenment, if not the cause of the totalitarianism as it emerged in Germany or the Soviet Union, has given rise to philosophical tendencies that have threatened the moral foundations of a free society. Polanyi rightly observes that although the Western world has opposed totalitarian tyrannies, the principle of freedom has been threatened and denigrated in more devious ways. Utilitarianism and pragmatism, in different ways, have declared thought to possess a legitimate function or significance only in relationship to human welfare largely in terms of physical material satisfactions; B. F. Skinner's behaviorism has reduced thought to various forms of conditioned behavior "beyond freedom and dignity"; existentialism fosters a view that there are no grounds for our choices except those we give ourselves.

While existentialists have rightly grasped the sense in which it is true that determinative reasons cannot be given for every choice, the way existentialists conceive of this fact has generated anti-intellectual attitudes with disastrous consequences for the very freedom they hold as being so fundamental. Polanyi presents a persuasive argument that the philosophical doubt and skepticism stemming from liberalism and the Enlightenment has fostered intellectual tendencies that, by denying the possibility of transcendent or universal standards of morality, leads quite logically to the conclusion that freedom of thought, itself, can claim no universal validity. It is not necessary to show that this implication leads inevitably to totalitarianism in order to sustain a contention that liberalism has not provided an adequate approach to defining the ethical foundations of a free society.

II

In challenging what he sees to be the nihilist implications in the rise of liberalism and the Enlightenment, Polanyi seeks to establish a concept of personal knowing that would overcome the dualism of objective vs. subjective, normative vs. descriptive that has been fostered by the tradition of scientific positivism. Central to his contention is that scien-

tific positivism has fostered a mechanistic view of
the world in which primary qualities could be brought
under control by Newtonian mechanics from which secondary qualities could be derived; the assumption that
scientific experience cannot go beyond the empirical
and that theory must be dropped the moment it
conflicts with observation; the effort to eliminate
from science all passionate, personal, and human
appraisals.[5]

Polanyi believes that this position has led to a
fundamental falsification of the nature of scientific
inquiry. Scientific method, in his view, cannot be
described as the application or verification of explicit rules and procedures or an objective criterion of
verification and testability. Scientific discovery
operates by selection, shaping and assimilating clues,
leaving to personal judgment an important role in
deciding what conflicting evidence invalidates a
proposition, what things coming to his notice must be
accepted as facts and what should be concluded from
them.[6]

It should be emphasized, however, that Polanyi is
not saying that the process of scientific discovery
does not involve adherence to particular rules and
procedures; but he emphasizes that these are only
"rules of art," and the application of a rule must
always rely ultimately upon acts not determined by
rule, where application leaves room for the exercise
of the personal judgment of the scientist. The process of scientific inquiry, then, is similar to any
kind of skillful performance that involves the incor-
poration of elements that are largely unspecifiable,
what Polanyi defines as a "subsidiary awareness" that
is not the object of focal attention.

What is involved here, then, is a dimension of
scientific discovery that is not a matter of applying
formal rules but an art that is learned through
apprenticeship to a master. It is the exercise of a skill
and the practice of connoisseurship in which the subsidiary awareness of particulars instrumental to a
skillful achievement function as the elements of an
observed comprehensive whole.[7] But Polanyi's concept
of the personal, it should be emphasized, is not a
defense of a radical subjectivity, for he clearly
distinguishes between the personal in us that actually
enters into commitments and the subjective states in
which we merely endure feelings.

46

The concept of the personal thus transcends the disjunction between subjective and objective. There is thus a correlation between the personal and the universal within the commitment situation: the scientist claims impersonal status to his judgments because he regards them as impersonally established by science. But it is precisely because of his submission to these standards that they can be said to exist for him; no man can know universal standards except by acknowledging their jurisdiction over him as part of the terms on which he holds himself responsible for pursuit of mental effort. Thus the scientist's intimation of a hidden reality is personal, but this is not equivalent to purely a subjective state of mind; it is a conviction held with a universal intent. This decision is not, therefore, irresponsible or arbitrary; he has arrived at his conclusion with the utmost exercise of responsibility.[8]

The emphasis upon the element of personal responsibility in scientific inquiry, Polanyi believes, indicates the presence of a moral element in the foundations of science, the faithfulness to an ideal that involves a matter of conscience. This cannot be fulfilled in abidance by rules but in the scientific conscience involved in the judgment of how far other people's data can be relied upon while avoiding at the same time the danger of too little or too much caution; in the sense of responsibility for the actions and claims he puts forth, in his personal commitment to the hidden reality of which he is predicting.[9] No matter how revolutionary the claim of the scientist may be, he will always meet any opposition of scientific opinion as he thinks it <u>is</u> to a scientific opinion as he thinks it <u>ought to be</u>. There is always an appeal to the tradition of science as a common ground between himself and his opponents, and they, in turn, would always accept this premise. When premises of science are held in common by the scientific community, each must subscribe to them as an act of devotion. They are not merely a guide to intuition but a guide to conscience; they are not merely indicative but normative.[10]

The political implications inherent in Polanyi's emphasis upon the moral character of scientific inquiry stem from his contention that the institutional structures and ideals of democracy are the fundamental premises of scientific inquiry: the art of free discussion, transmitted by a tradition of civil liberty and embodied in the institutions of democracy.

A community pledged to seek the truth cannot fail to accord freedom to science as one form of that truth.

> Thus while we recognize that true propositions cannot be established by explicit criteria, we do assert the universal validity of propositions to which we personally assent. Therein is expressed our conviction that truth is real and cannot fail to be recognized by those who generally seek it; and our belief in a free society as an organization of its members consciences for the fulfillment of their inherent obligation to the truth.[11]

In his contention that a free society provides the premises of scientific inquiry, Polanyi emphasizes that this does not mean a wholly open society, for a free society embodies a traditional framework. In the case of science, for example, the freedom to make an original contribution rests upon traditional beliefs enforced by a community of scientists that make for continuity in both discipline and innovation and brings them together. The scientist acts under judgment of a reality with which he is seeking to establish contact. While his acts are intensely personal, there is no self-will in them. Originality is guided by a sense of responsibility for advancing the cause of truth. The pursuit of science involves acts of personal judgment with a view to a reality with which it is seeking to establish contact. The free society is thus not simply an open one in which anything goes.

> It is a society in which men being engaged in various activities whose ends are considered worthy of respect, are allowed the freedom to pursue these ends. A free society is therefore one whose citizens in the main are committed to--dedicated to--various ideal ends (such as truth) and therefore one that is able to respect the free activities of its citizens in pursuit of such ends. It cannot be a free society by being open on matters such as these, that is by being neutral with respect to truth and falsehood, justice and injustice, honesty and fraud.[12]

III

Where Polanyi's perspective becomes more problematical and controversial is in regard to his defense

48

of the economic individualism inherent in the concept of the market economy. It is here that one finds a central paradox of Polanyi's political theory: on the one hand a powerful attack upon what he sees to be the nihilist implications of Enlightenment rationalism as a radical skepticism and doubt towards traditional spiritual authority, and yet an equally strong defense of what is the direct product of Enlightenment rationalism, the spontaneous, self-adjusting mechanism of the market economy. This paradox would appear to stem from Polanyi's conviction that the moral obligations that are intrinsic to the activities of the scientist, scholar, or judge do not apply to individuals engaged in economic activity where the motivations of profit maximization and competitive advantage are intrinsic to the automatic, self-adjusting mechanism of the market economy. This system is jeopardized by any restraint or interference on the basis of moral considerations of a public interest or a concept of economic planning.

In evaluating this contention, it is necessary to distinguish between what it embodies as an empirical as opposed to a normative-ethical judgment. Polanyi's argument, at the empirical level, embodies the contention that central planning is impossible because it violates the principle of an effective "span of control," that it exceeds the number of subordinates that can be effectively controlled by any one superior.[13] Any industrial system, he contends, involves the allocation to each plant of materials produced by other plants and a daily adjustment of these allocations of materials in response from other plants and consumers. If this had to be directed centrally, it could not satisfy the requirements of an effective span of control and thus could not function. There can be mutual adjustments, but this must not go beyond a certain limit; such adjustments may condition the actions of subordinates but must never determine them. The fallacies of central planning, Polanyi argues, are conclusively demonstrated in the economic disaster that occurred in the Soviet Union in the 1919-1921 period, a disaster that was finally retrieved only by the resort to capitalist methods.

Polanyi believes that for any national body to aim at totals of so many bushels of wheat harvested, barrels of oil refined, and so on, is without meaning.

A particular sum of outputs could be rationally desired only in view of the

49

reasons which make individual managers decide, after weighing up all alternative lines of production, on the sizes of the individual outputs constituting the sum. But the adding up of individual outputs to a production target eliminates all the proper reasons for which the individual plant managers might decide to produce such outputs as would add up to the totals set out in the plan, and there is then no reason left why these totals should be desired, nor any sense in planning them to be of any particular size.[14]

Mutual adjustments between businessmen, Polanyi believes, are primarily guided by a striving for individual advantage. The success of industrial production undertaken to satisfy consumer demand must be tested by consumer satisfaction, and the only test of this is the willingness to buy in a competitive market at prices that give profit to producers.

The difficulty of Polanyi's analysis, at the level of empirical criteria, is simply that it is not adequately supported by actual historical evidence. Polanyi cites only the failure of Soviet central planning in 1921 as evidence that centralized planning is impossible. But this ignores the record of Soviet economic planning since the post-World War II era. While there is wide agreement on evidence of inefficiencies in Soviet planning in regard to consumer goods, bottlenecks, hoarding of capital goods, low productivity in agriculture, and so forth, it is by no means obvious that Soviet planning has been a total failure.[15] Although clearly behind the United States, the Soviet Union represents one-fifth of the industrial output of the entire globe. While living standards remain behind the United States and Western European economies, the percentage differences have been narrowing. The Soviet record, in the view of some observers, is particularly well suited to relatively less developed economies embarked on crash industrial programs: the harnessing of unused resources, imposing forced savings, and bringing about expansion primarily by net addition to plant equipment and to the industrial labor force.[16]

But even if one were to concede that the Soviet Union demonstrates the inefficiencies or inadequacies of central planning, it does not follow that the only alternative is an economic system founded on premises of the free market economy, for such a conclusion fails to take into account the contemporary historical experience of countries that represent varying mixtures of economic planning and market principles ranging from the liberalized Marxism of Yugoslavia, the democratic socialism of Sweden and France, to the state capitalism of Japan. The specifics of how these countries exemplify a mixture of free market principles along with economic planning is beyond the scope of this essay. The essential point to be made here is that contemporary historical experience does not warrant Polanyi's contention that satisfactory economic performance is not possible where market principles are subject to restraints and modifications in terms of economic planning priorities.

The central issue in regard to free market economy vs. state economic planning, however, is not ultimately a question of technical-quantitative criteria about levels of productivity. Rather it is a normative issue of what a democratic society requires in terms of the relationship of individual freedom to the public interest. Polanyi is on sound ground in his contention that both scientific and humanistic inquiry must be protected against the danger of state control. Polanyi's position in this respect is clearly recognized by the First Amendment of the American Constitution. But this cannot mean that there are not areas of human inquiry that cannot be subject to restrictions in terms of a concept of the public interest. Some of the long-standing issues of American constitutional history pertaining to defamation of character, obscenity, threats to public security could be considered in this light.[17]

Insofar as economic activity is concerned, Polanyi is fully cognizant of the dangers of a doctrinaire economic individualism. He acknowledges that the worst forms of destructive behavior and human exploitation have been in the name of individual self-assertion. He acknowledges (as previously noted) the moral legitimacy of the demands for reforms that opened the way for the English, American, and French revolutions, the liberation of slavery, factory reforms, and such. In considering developments of the contemporary period, Polanyi recognizes that the consequences of commercial activities that lead to environmental pollution and ill health require government regulation; such regulation he would see as negative rather than prescriptive, restricting the range of commercial activities by outlawing unsocial transactions. But he also recognizes the necessity of a

51

more positive role of the state in the areas of education and social amenities that cannot be supplied by commercial sources. Yet Polanyi insists that this does not affect the substance of his contention that the major parts of the productive system must ignore the "diffuse effects" of its own activity.[18] Thus he does not appear to see any inconsistency between acknowledgment of the reforms of the past one hundred years that have made such an important contribution to modern civilization and his contention that the individualist, profit making motives inherent in the market economy must be free from any concept of a public interest imposed by state authority.

What Polanyi fails to recognize on this point is that the spiritual foundation of Western democracy, to which he pays homage, embodies a concept of a common good that is in fundamental antagonism to the classical liberal concept of the market economy. This heritage was given its most classical formulation in the synthesis of Aristotle with Christian faith affected by St. Thomas Aquinas: the view of political society as an association of individuals for pursuit of the good life, the recognition of the moral purpose of government and political authority conducted in accordance with the rule of law. The meaning of this tradition, as an opposition to the tenets of classical liberalism, has been well articulated in Papal encyclicals since Rerum Novarum.

A recent encyclical of Pope John Paul II, On Human Work, shows the continuity with this tradition. The Christian tradition, although opposed to Marxist collectivism, has never upheld the absolute right to property of capitalist theory. On the contrary, it has always understood this right within a broader context of the rights of all to use the goods of creation; the right of property is subordinate to the right to common use. From this point of view, in fact, one cannot exclude the socialization, in suitable conditions, of certain means of production. But socialism would not mean merely converting the means of production into state property. It would mean a system that would associate labor with the ownership of capital and produce intermediate bodies--economic, social, and political--that would have real autonomy in regard to public powers, pursuing specific interests in subordination to demands of the public good.[19]

The emphasis upon political democracy as the pursuit of a common good embodies a concept of economic planning that would seek to avoid both the dangers of a totalitarian collectivism as well as the atomistic individualism of the market economy. The essential spirit of this position has been eloquently articulated by an outstanding representative of the democratic temper of a quarter century ago--Karl Mannheim.

> Our task is to build a social system by planning, but planning of a special kind: it must be _planning for freedom_, subjected to democratic control; _planning, but_ not _restrictionist_ so as to favor group monopolies either of entrepreneurs or workers associations, but "planning for plenty", i.e., full employment and full exploitation of resources; _planning for social justice_ rather than absolute equality, with differentiation of rewards and status on the basis of genuine equality rather than privilege; _planning for cultural standards_ without "leveling down"--a planned transition making for progress without discarding what is valuable in tradition; _planning that counteracts the dangers of a mass society_ by coordination of the means of social control but interfering only in cases of institutional or moral deterioration defined by collective criteria; _planning for balance_ between centralization and dispersion of power; _planning_ for gradual transformation of society _in order to encourage the growth of personality_; in short, _planning, but not regimentation._[20]

IV

The failure of Polanyi's political theory as a defense of the classical model of the market economy does not diminish the value of his contribution to the task of defining the moral imperatives of a free society in terms that would seek to avoid both the inadequacies of classical metaphysics as well as the intellectual premises of Enlightenment rationalism. What is central in this contribution is Polanyi's concept of personal knowing as a corrective to the dualisms of subjective vs. objective, knowing vs. valuing, reason vs. faith that have been engendered by Enlightenment rationalism; a belief that the normative ideals of a free society--truth, justice, and charity--are the premises of both scientific and humanistic inquiry and that these ideals have a transcendent authority within a tradition of Western Christendom.

While Polanyi fails to see that this heritage embodies a concept of a common good in antagonism to the radical individualism of the market economy, his attack upon the intellectual premises of Enlightenment rationalism actually contributes to this conclusion. Polanyi's perspective also contributes to the recognition that while the normative ideals of democracy are rooted in the spiritual sources of Western civilization, this recognition must not mean the repudiation of what has been of value in the rise of liberalism and the Enlightenment as a force upon problems of social change and reform. Polanyi recognizes that the pre-Enlightenment era of dogmatic authority and the indifference of the traditional Church to social evils is not acceptable. Polanyi (as previously noted) is fully congizant of the moral aspirations of the age of reason that opened the way for the English, American, and French revolutions, the liberation of slaves, factory reforms, and such, in which public opinion was swayed by charity, the desire for justice, and the detestation of social evil.

His point is simply that these moral aspirations did not have a grounding in the radical skepticism and utilitarian-materialist philosophies of the era and were actually a continuing legacy of traditional ideals that stem from Western Christendom. Polanyi's concept of personal knowledge thus provides a fruitful framework for the development of a type of Christian humanism that embodies implications that Polanyi does not himself fully realize: a Christian humanism that would reject both a doctrinaire totalitarian collectivism as well as the doctrinaire individualism of the market economy in favor of a concept of a constitutional polity as the exercise of freedom in terms of subordination to the common good.

1. Majorie Green, The Knower and the Known (New York: Basic Books, 1966), p. 152.

2. Michael Polanyi and Harry Prosch, Meaning (Chicago: University of Chicago Press, 1975), p. 7.

3. Ibid., p. 10.

4. Ibid., p. 19.

5. Michael Polanyi, Personal Knowledge (New York: Harper & Row, 1962), p. 9.

6. Michael Polanyi, Science, Faith and Society (Chicago: University fo Chicago Press, 1964), p. 11.

7. Polanyi, Personal Knowledge, pp. 64, 65.

8. Ibid., p. 311.

9. Polanyi, Science, Faith and Society, pp. 39, 40.

10. Ibid., p. 64.

11. Ibid., p. 73.

12. Polanyi and Prosch, p. 197.

13. Michael Polanyi, The Logic of Liberty (Chicago: University of Chicago Press, 1969), p. 112.

14. Ibid., p. 136.

15. For an excellent symposium on this question see The Soviet Crucible, edited by Samuel Hendel (Belmont, Calif.: Dusbury Press, 1980), chap. 6.

16. Harry G. Shaffer, "Soviet Economic Performance in Historical Perspective," in The Soviet Crucible, pp. 301-304.

17. For a brilliant elaboration on this thesis see Hadley Arkers, The Philosopher in the City (Princeton, N.J.: Princeton University Press, 1981), chaps. 1, 2, 3.

18. Polanyi, The Logic of Liberty, p. 149.

19. "Laborem Exercens," On Human Work, Third
Encyclical of Pope John Paul II, from Origins, NC
documentary service (September 24, 1981), pp. 235-236.

20. Karl Mannheim, Freedom, Power and Democratic
Planning (New York: Oxford University Press, 1950),
p. 29.

CHAPTER 4

THE CRITICAL THEORY OF JURGEN HABERMAS

The hermeneutical theories of Gadamer and Taylor, as considered in previous chapters, are greatly indebted to the classical Aristotelian concept of praxis as an interpretation of the relationship of universals to particular situations and the concept of human language as a horizon of hermeneutical ontology. With Habermas we find a concept of praxis nourished by the classical Aristotelian model but concerned with a critical theory that would overcome what he sees to be the metaphysical aspects of the Aristotelian heritage as well as its association with conservative political implications.

Habermas has been commonly viewed as a protege of the Frankfurt School of critical social theory that emerged in the early part of the century associated with Theodore Adorno and Max Horkheimer.[1] Central in this development was a general disenchantment with Marxist orthodoxy that the development of capitalism would create both objective and subjective conditions for a radical transformation. Although accepting the general validity of Marxist critique of political economy, the Frankfort School placed emphasis upon the social cultural dimensions neglected by orthodox Marxism, especially what they saw to be a rationalization process or "instrumental reason" leading to the total political and administrative domination of social life techniques developed and stabilized by institutions as the military, bureaucracy, business, and the "culture industry." By the 1940s the failure of the labor movement, the ascendancy of Stalinism in Russia, postwar stabilization of capitalism lessened confidence that the forces of production could be a basis for liberation. The development of "administered societies" in Eastern Europe called Marxist theory into even deeper question.

What was becoming apparent to the Frankfurt theorists was that the ascendancy of an instrumental rationality in modern industrial societies was calling into question the very structure of Western rationalism, and the Enlightenment project of a liberated humanity was turning into its opposite--a new and powerful force for domination. During the 1960s Herbert Marcuse became well known for his concept of "one dimensional" thought in which the growth of forces of production fueled by scientific and technological development was leading to a totally rationalized society where freedom and personal autonomy is impossible.

Habermas can be seen as a continuation of the project of the Frankfurt School as the effort to separate the distortions of the Enlightenment from its real advances so as to save its goal of human liberation. Habermas has characterized his position as a "reconstruction of historical materialism," recognizing the value of Marxist understanding of the material basis of human evolution but emphasizing the Marxist failure to give adequate recognition of learning processes that give rise to moral-practical consciousness decisive for structures of communicative action. A central theme in the critical social theory of Habermas is the concept of a communicative rationality based on argumentative speech in which participants seek to assure themselves of both the unity of the objective world and the intersubjectivity of their life world as distinct from a cognitive-instrumental rationality concerned with efficiency of means-ends relationships in adaptation to a contingent environment.

It would be impossible within the frame of this essay to do justice to the wide-ranging philosophical, sociological analysis that characterizes the writings of Habermas over a period of many years. The intent here will be to focus upon what critics have seen to be a central tension between "Kantian transcendental" vs. Marxist presupposition in his critical theory. In his more recent writings Habermas has sought to overcome this difficulty through a concept of communicative rationality assimilating insights of speech act theory and the developmental psychology of Piaget. Critical response to his present work raises serious doubts as to the success of this effort. But it is the thesis of this essay that Habermas makes an important contribution within the framework of a critical dialogue with Hans Gadamer that has been well articulated by Paul Ricoeur. While this would recognize the centrality of historical consciousness in opposition to the presuppositions of Enlightenment rationalism, it would acknowledge a "distanciation" within historical consciousness that gives place for a critical reflection that challenges the dogmatism of tradition and that encompasses the human interest in liberation and emancipation.

The tension between Marxist and Kantian perspectives in the critical theory of Habermas is most clearly apparent in his early book, <u>Knowledge and Human Interests</u>. While Habermas affirms the Marxist emphasis upon the understanding of thought within the natural evolution of the human species, he objects to the Marxist reduction of human reflection to the process of production. The inadequacy of Marxism, in this respect, is that it does not recognize the specific meaning of a science of man as a critique of ideology in distinction from an instrumental meaning of science.[2] Thus he does not take account of the fact that the liberating aspects of communicative action do not stem directly through productive activity but rather through the revolutionary activity of struggling classes and the critical activity of the reflective sciences.[3]

In the view of Habermas, the raising of the productivity of technically exploitable knowledge, which in substitution of machinery for men has its counterpart in the self-reflection of consciousness that has reached to a level of critique and freed itself from all ideological delusions. While these two developments are interdependent, they do not converge. "Marx tried in vain to capture this in a dialectic of forces of production and relations of production. In vain-- for the meaning of this 'dialectics' must remain unclarified as long as the materialist concept of the synthesis of man and nature is restricted to the categorical framework of production."[4]

Habermas believes that there is thus a peculiar disproportion in the writings of Marx between the practice of inquiry and the limited philosophical self-understanding of this inquiry. In his empirical analysis he comprehends the history of the species under categories of material activity and the critical abolition of ideologies, instrumental action, revolutionary practice, labor, and reflection. "But Marx interprets what he does in the more restricted conception of the species self-reflection through work alone."[5]

Habermas' approach to defining the foundations of a more adequate critical theory may be seen as a "reconstructive materialism." The keynote of this reconstruction is the relationship between "knowledge and interest" that is able to encompass the Marxist emphasis upon instrumental knowledge associated with the process of production but also the dimension of symbolic interaction and cultural tradition. The concept of "interest," Habermas emphasizes, is not meant to imply a naturalistic reduction of transcendental properties to empirical ones. Knowledge-constitutive interests, he contends, mediate the natural history of the human species with the logic of its self-formative process. "I term interest the basic orientation rooted in specific fundamental conditions of the possible reproduction and self constitution of the human species; namely work and interaction. Hence, these basic orientations do not aim at the gratification of immediately empirical need, but at the solution of system problems in general."[6]

Knowledge-constitutive interests can be defined as th function of objectively constituted problems of the preservation of life that have been solved by the cultural forms of existence. Work and interaction, by nature, include processes of learning and arriving at mutual understanding. This is why knowledge-constitutive interest rooted in work and interaction cannot be comprehended in the biological frame of reference of the reproduction and preservation of the species.

> Thus, knowledge-constitutive interests would be completely misunderstood if viewed as mere functions of the reproduction of social life. Cognitive interest is, therefore, a peculiar category which conforms as little to the distinction between empirical and transcendental or factual and symbolic determinations as to that between motivation and cognition. For knowledge is neither a mere instrument of an organism's adaptation to a changing environment nor the action of a pure rational being removed from the context of life in contemplation.[7]

Habermas perceives a correlation between knowledge-constitutive interests and processes of inquiry at three levels: a technical cognitive interest related to the empirical-analytical sciences, a practical cognitive interest related to the historical-hermeneutical sciences, a critical social theory that incorporates an emancipatory cognitive interest.[8]

In the empirical analytic sciences, Habermas contends, theories are seen as comprising hypothetic-deductive connections of propositions, permitting the deduction of law-like hypotheses with empirical content. Empirical-analytical knowledge is thus possible predictive knowledge involving controlled observation, providing immediate evidence without any admixture of subjectivity. Thus, theories of empirical science disclose a reality subject to a constitutive interest in the technical control of objectified processes.[9]

In the historical-hermeneutic sciences, however, the validity of propositions is not constituted in the form of reference to technical control; formalized language and objectified experience have not yet been divorced. Access to facts is provided by the understanding of meaning, not observation. The rules of hermeneutics determine the possible meaning of the validity statements in the cultural sciences. Hermeneutical knowledge is always mediated through the preunderstanding derived from the interpreter's initial situation. The interpreter's own world becomes changed at the same time as a traditional world discloses itself to the interpreter. There is, thus, a communication between both worlds. The subject of understanding comprehends the substantive content of tradition by applying tradition to himself and his situation. Hermeneutical inquiry thus discloses a reality subject to a constitutive interest in the preservation and expansion of intersubjectivity of possible action-oriented mutual understanding. "The understanding of meaning is directed in its very structure towards the attainment of possible consensus among actors in the framework of a self-understanding derived from tradition. This we shall call the practical cognitive interest in contrast to the technical."[10]

The distinction made by Habermas between a technical interest of the empirical sciences versus the practical interest of the hermeneutical sciences takes on important political implications in his contention that since the end of the eighteenth century the emergence of the social sciences and the disciplines of jurisprudence have "drawn off the waters" of classical politics. The establishment of political science in the mode of the experimental sciences has little in common more than the name with the old politics. This development occurred with the rejection of the classical tradition by Thomas Hobbes, completing a whole manner of thinking initiated by Machiavelli on the one side and Thomas More on the other. In this development, Habermas observes, three aspects of the classical version of politics have been rejected: politics as the practice of the just life and the continuation of ethics, the concept of politics as a praxis in opposition to techne as the expert mastery of objectified tasks, the claim that politics and practical philosophy cannot be compared to knowledge with a rigorous science.[11]

In his consideration of the contribution of classical politics, it would be important to emphasize that Habermas is not referring to the pure theory of "Ideas" of the Platonic heritage but rather to the praxis political theory associated with Aristotle. The traditional ideal of praxis, Habermas contends, has been replaced by the ascendancy of scientifically grounded social philosophy where human behavior is to be considered the material of science disregarding categories of ethical-social intercourse. What characterizes the passage from traditional to modern society is calling into question traditional forms of legitimacy and power. The older myths, religious-metaphysical world views, obeyed a logic of interactive contexts answering central questions of man's collective existence and individual life history. "Their themes are justice and freedom, violence and oppression; happiness and gratification; poverty, illness and death."[12]

But the contemporary ethos of technological rationality, Habermas contends, embodies a rationalization of means and ends associated with strategy and action. This process, he believes, has had a profound effect upon the nature of politics. The old style politics through traditional forms of legitimacy defined itself in relationship to practical goals where the "good life" was defined in terms of interactive relationships. But contemporary trends under the ascendency of a technological rationality are aimed at the function of a manipulative system eliminating practical questions and the necessity of discussing standards. The solution of technical problems is not seen as depending on public discussion. A new politics of state intervention requires, in fact, a "depolitization" of the masses of the population. The scientization of politics has become a pervasive feature of the modern era facilitated by rewards under government control and scientific consultation to public services.[13]

Habermas clearly believes that the ascendancy of a technological rationality associated with the empirical-analytical sciences has eroded the positive features in the practical interest associated with the historical-hermeneutical sciences as the understanding of meaning directed towards the attainment of consensus among actors in the framework of a self-understanding derived from tradition. Habermas thus recognizes the value of the traditional ideal of praxis insofar as it provides a focus upon normative questions of the good life. But Habermas also stresses the inadequacy of this ideal insofar as it became the basis for equating legitimacy with customs that are the source of unjust or oppressive social structures. It is for this reason that a critical social theory cannot be satisfied with the practical interest associated with the hermeneutical sciences; for a critical social theory is concerned with how frozen relationships may be transformed. The meaning and validity of critical propositions are established by the concept of "self-reflection." "The latter releases the subject from dependency on hypostatized powers. Self-reflection is determined by an emancipatory cognitive interest. Critical oriented sciences share this interest with philosophy."[14]

Habermas observes, finally, that in the power of self-reflection, knowledge and interest are one. But only in an emancipated society where autonomy and responsibility have been realized would communication be developed into universal priority of nonauthoritative development in which truth statements can be based on the anticipation of the good life.[15]

Critical objection to Habermas' theory of knowledge constitutive interests has centered principally on the tension between its Marxian and Kantian components. The concept of self-reflection, it has been noted, embodies a Kantian transcendental presupposition as the condition of the possibility of knowledge. But Habermas is employing the concept of reflection in a Marxist sense as the critique of ideology aiming at freeing the subject from dependency on "hypostatized powers" concealed in structures of speech and action. But in the view of Richard Bernstein this is to make an unwarranted identification between reflection and practical engagement, and to identify the two interests is to succumb to an idealist illusion.[16]

Perhaps the more basic difficulty in the critical theory of Habermas, as Thomas McCarthy contends, is simply that the attempt to combine a quasi-transcendental theory of knowledge with a naturalistic approach to subjective conditions of knowledge involves Habermas in a basic dilemma. On the one hand he wants to speak of the interest of knowledge that can claim a transcendental status: the work and interaction that involves processes of learning and arriving at mutual understanding that cannot be comprehended in a biological framework of the reproduction and preservation of the species. On the other hand Habermas ascribes to the subject of knowledge not only the intelligible character of a community that constitutes the world from a transcendental perspective but also the empirical character of the species that has emerged in the natural evolution of the species.[17]

II

Habermas has been well aware of the tension between Kantian transcendental vs. Marxist aspects of his culture theory, and his recent writings have shown an effort to resolve this problem culminating in his current work, The Theory of Communicative Action. In this work Habermas emphasizes that philosophy can no longer make any pretension to a tolalizing knowledge, and what it can accomplish within its reflective competence is within the framework of scientific conventions; it has become "metaphilosophy." All attempts at discovery of a "First Philosophy" or transcendental a priori constructs of human consciousness have broken down. Habermas believes there is now a prospect for convergence of philosophy and sciences towards the point of a theory of rationality.[18] His current work, as the attempt to realize this objective, embodies the effort to formulate a concept of communicative rationality that draws upon implication of speech act theory, the developmental psychology of Piaget, and sociological concepts of rationalization in contributions of Max Weber, Max Horkheimer, Theodore Adorno, Herbert Mead, and others.

A general concept of rationality, Habermas believes, must seek to establish a distinction between a cognitive-instrumental rationality vs. a communicative rationality. A cognitive-instrumental rationality, he contends, has to do with successful self-maintenance or intelligent adaptation to environment. A communicative rationality, by contrast, "carries with it connotations based ultimately on the central experience of the unconstrained unifying consensus-bringing force of argumentative speech in which different participants overcome their merely subjective views and owing to the mutuality of rationally motivated conviction assuring themselves of both the unity of the objective world and the inter-subjectivity of their life world."[19]

The analysis of rationality thus begins with the concept of propositional knowledge of the objective world, but there are differences in the way knowledge is used. From one perspective a _telos_ inherent in rationality appears in instrumental rationality, from the other communicative understanding. Through communicative practice, acting subjects assure themselves of a common life situation and an intersubjectively shared life world as a totality of interpretations presupposed by members as a background knowledge. Well-grounded assertions of efficient action are certainly a sign of rationality, but there are other types of expression that can have good reasons, even though not tied to truth as success claims, having to do with desires or intuitions, feelings, or moods. Normatively regulated actions and expressive self-presentations are understandable in their context and connected with criticizable validity claims, but the reference is to norms of subjective experience rather than facts. The knowledge involved in normatively regulated action or expressive manifestations does not refer to the existence of a state of affairs but to validity of norms or to the manifestations of subjective experience.[20]

Building on implications of action theory in the social sciences, Habermas contends that speakers claim truth for statements or existential presuppositions, rightness for legitimately regulated actions and their normative context, and truthfulness or sincerity for the manifestation of subjective experiences. This involves recognition of three relations of actor to the world presupposed by the social scientist, but in the concept of communicative action they are ascribed to the speakers themselves: that is the "fit" or "mis-fit" between utterances and (1) the objective world as the totality of all entities about which true statements are possible, (2) the social world as the totality of all legitimately regulated impersonal relations, (3) the subjective world as the totality of the experiences of the speaker to which he has privileged access.[21]

The concept of rationality proper to communicative practice points to the practice of argumentation as a court of appeal in reference to unclarified universal validity claims. Argumentation has to do with that type of speech in which participants thematize contested validity claims and attempt to vindicate or criticize them through arguments. This process would go along with an emphasis upon exposure to criticism and ability to learn from mistakes. Moral argument, moreover, involves a strong presupposition that a grounded consensus can, in principle, be achieved where norms of action appear in the domain of validity with a claim to matters that involve an interest common to all those affected that deserve to be recognized.[22]

Habermas recognizes that attempts to elucidate a concept of rationality are anchored in the preunderstanding of a Western world view. This makes it necessary to make comparisons with mythical understanding of traditional societies that are in sharp contrast to understanding of Western modernity. Habermas gives attention to the anthropological interpretation associated with Peter Winch who argues that the categories of linguistic analysis emerging from Wittgenstein must be applied to Western interpretation of alien cultures. World views share the cultural knowledge with the help of which a language community interprets the world. True and untrue are thus concepts inherent in language. The Azande and the anthropologist, for example, speak different languages and the anthropologist has no right to judge beliefs in witches and magic by standards of Western rationality.[23]

Habermas accepts Winch's emphasis upon linguistically articulated world views and forms of life, but he believes it is possible to establish an independent standard of rationality as "open vs. closed"--the readiness to learn and the openness to criticism that are the outstanding features of the scientific spirit.

Habermas finds support for this position in the learning theory of Piaget who in describing levels of learning ability emphasizes that in the transition to a new stage, the interpretation of superceded stages is categorically devalued. The growing child works out concepts of external and internal worlds in dealing with objects and him or herself, a distinction between physical objects and dealing with social objects, that is, a "reciprocal action between subject and object and other subjects." Correspondingly, the external universe is differentiated into the world of perceptible and manipulative objects and the world of normative interpersonal relationships. Cognitive development signifies in general the decentration of egocentric understanding of the world. "Every action oriented or reaching understanding can be considered as part of the cooperative process of interpretation aimed at situation definitions that are intersubjectively recognized."[24]

Habermas introduces at this point the concept of a "lifeworld" as the background convictions that supply definitions presupposed by participants. The lifeworld is a storehouse of interpretive works of preceding generations, which acts as a conservative counterweight to disagreement in the process of reaching understanding in regard to criticizable validity claims.

But with decentration of world views there is less need for understanding that is predecided by the interpreted background of the lifeworld and where participants themselves have the possibility of examining grounds for yes/no positions.

> To the degree the lifeworld of social groups is interpreted through mutual world views, the burden of interpretation is removed from the individual member, as well as the change for him to bring about an agreement open to criticism. To the extent that the world view remains sociocentric, in Piaget's terms, it does not permit differentiation between the world of existing states of affairs, valid norms, and expressible subjective experiences. The linguistic world view is reified as the world order and cannot reach the critical zone in which communicatively achieved agreement depends upon autonomous yes/no responses to criticizable validity claims.[25]

Habermas emphasizes that the cultural tradition must make available formal concepts for the objective, social, and subjective worlds; it must differentiate validity claims (propositional truth, normative rightness, subjective truthfulness) as well as basic attitudes (objectifying, norm conformative, and expressive). The cultural tradition must also permit a reflective relation to itself so that it can be stripped of dogmatism in order to permit the interpretations stored in tradition to be placed in question and subjected to critical revision. This requires cognitive activities having to do with learning process guided by hypothesis and filtered through argumentation in the domain of objectifying thought, moral practical insight, and aesthetic perception.[26]

Piaget's concept of decentration, Habermas believes, thus helps to clarify the connection between the structure of world views, the lifeworld as a context of the process of understanding, and the possibility of rational conduct of life embodied in the concept of a communicative rationality. "This concept relates a decentered understanding of the world to the possibility of discursively redeeming criticizable validity claims."[27]

Much of the remainder of his massive two-volume study involves an appropriation and critique of the contributions of such figures as Herbert Mead, Talcott Parsons, and others in regard to the historical process of rationalization as a transition from traditional societies to modernity that cannot be considered in the frame of this chapter. It will suffice to provide a broad outline of what emerges from this analysis in terms of what Habermas contributes as a continuation of the Frankfurt School of critical theory.

In his previous writings, as already noted, Habermas stressed the deficiencies of Marxism as an overemphasis upon the mode of production and the failure to give recognition to learning processes that give rise to moral-practical consciousness decisive for communicative action. The practical intent of Marx, he contends, can be preserved only by freeing historical materialism from the perspective of scientific-technical-instrumental reason. Central to this reconstruction is the concept of lifeworld, a prereflective context for language that stands behind the back of each participant in communication and supports the process of understanding. What has been peculiar to the process of the transition from traditional society to modernity has been the progressive "rationalization" of the lifeworld in terms of differentiation of value spheres, the institutionalization of argumentation, and the secularization of norms. This involves a distinction between the more or less differentiated or rationalized lifeworld reproduced by communicative actions vs. the more formal organized systems of action at the level of state and administration reproduced by purposive action.

Economic and administrative systems, Habermas contends, are anchored in the lifeworld just as in Marx

the superstructure is anchored in the base. The difference is that the base for Marx is the paradigm of
production where for Habermas it is the lifeworld
understood in terms of communication. Habermas emphasizes an interaction between the lifeworld and the
social system. The lifeworld depends upon the social
system both in terms of material production and the
state organization. The social system depends upon
the lifeworld for both the reproduction of socialized
individuals and the continuation of coherent cultural
traditions. They are thus interdependent and interact
in complex ways in the course of social development.

In the process of modernization, Habermas
believes, the social system becomes more differentiated and complex, while the lifeworld becomes more
rationalized. The differentiation of value spheres
(science, morality, art) characteristic of modernity
may be viewed as normal and even progressive, allowing
for critical appropriation of tradition, argumentation, and consensus. But there is a dark side, in
that capitalist economic development and the modern
administrative state have imposed a scientific technological rationality over other value spheres, leading
to loss of meaning, anomie, and personal disorders
that Habermas speaks of as "a colonization of the
lifeworld." The concept of communicative rationality
central to context of the lifeworld thus becomes the
normative foundation for criticizing the one-sided
rationality of capitalist society.

Habermas addresses himself, finally, to a problem
that is a return to his earlier writings on questions
of the relation of theory to practice and the problem
of what social agents can realize the emancipative
critical goals of theory. The nature of conflict in
advanced capitalism, he believes, has changed in the
past several decades. Unlike the "old politics" that
centered on questions of economic, domestic, and military security, the "new politics" centers on questions
of life, participation, and human rights. While the
old politics was supported by entrepreneurs, workers,
and the professional middle class, the new politics is
supported by the new middle class, the young, and
those groups with higher levels of formal education.
Habermas discerns here a line of conflict between
social strata more directly involved in the production
process and an interest in maintaining capital growth
as opposed to groups at the periphery more sensitive
to the self-destructive consequences of uncontrolled
growth and technical administrative domination. This

includes the peace movement, antinuclear and environmental movement, minority liberation movements, and
the women's movement. While not all these groups are
progressive or contain emancipatory potential, they
are at least united in resistance to colonization of
the lifeworld. Habermas sees the practical intentions
of a reformulated critical theory in terms of
encouraging an offensive and universalistic posture on
the part of these groups that can aid in focusing the
struggle against a one-sided capitalist rationality
that denies the possibility of constructing a society
of undistorted communication and free equal
participation.

III

In evaluating the critical theory of Habermas the
crucial question is whether his recent work has overcome the incompatible tension between Kantian vs.
Marxist features that critics saw to be the failure of
his previous writings. Habermas' effort in this
direction, it has been seen, involves the attempt to
develop a concept of a communicative rationality assimilating the implications of speech act theory, the
developmental psychology of Piaget, and concepts of
rationality from the contributions of Max Weber,
Herbert Mead, and others. Habermas is thus making an
effort to develop a reconstructive science as a move
away from the transcendental presuppositions of his
earlier writings. In the view of Rick Roderick,
however, Habermas has still not "detranscendentalized"
his project. His reconstructive-empirical approach is
still transcendental as an examination of the conditions for the possibility of thought.

> Habermas' concept of communicative rationa-
> lity as a critical standard that is both par-
> tially transcendental and partially imminent
> is a complex and subtle attempt to find a
> normative basis for a critical theory of the
> kind he believes is required. In the end,
> however, Habermas remains trapped in the same
> dilemma he faced earlier in his "quasi-
> transcendental interest." Once one has
> accepted the "inside-outside" dichotomy, it
> is impossible to go down the middle. The
> foundation is either external or internal, is
> either in society and history or it is not.[28]

The above criticism points up some serious difficulties in the critical theory of Habermas, but it

does not put into fair perspective both the value and
limitations of his contribution. Such a perspective
has been effectively articulated by Paul Ricoeur in
his arbitration of the debate between Gadamer and
Habermas that was briefly noted in Chapter 1. While
Ricoeur is generally sympathetic to Gadamer's hermeneutical theory, he believes it is possible to overcome the opposition between a "hermeneutic of
tradition" and a "critique of ideology" in terms of
the contention that the consciousness of historical
efficacity contains within itself a moment of
"distanciation." "Historical efficacity is efficacity
at a distance, which makes the distant near. Without
the tension between the self and the other, there is
no historical consciousness."

The dialectic of participation and distanciation,
Ricoeur contends, is the key to Gadamer's "fusion of
horizons" as the communication of present with the
past. This makes possible communication at a distance
between two different situational consciousnesses.
"We do not live, therefore, within closed horizons or
within a unique horizon. The tension between the self
and the other, between the near and the far, is
accomplished on the distant horizon.[29] The essential
linguisticality of historical experience is intrinsic
to the distanciation in the interior of participation.
For linguisticality signifies that my belonging to a
tradition is through the interpretation of signs,
texts in which cultural heritages are inscribed and
are offered for our interpretation. Thus, our communication at a distance is an "issue of text" that no
longer belongs either to its author or to the
reader.[30]

Ricoeur believes that the process of hermeneutical
interpretation gives a place for the role of critical
social sciences that the historical hermeneutical
sciences must acknowledge. For while the historical-
hermeneutical sciences are founded on the centrality
of language, there must be a recognition of the
intertwining of work-power-language.

> The very fact that linguisticality should be
> subordinate to historical experience and to
> aesthetic experience is sufficient warning
> that language is only the locus for the artic-
> ulation of an experience which supports it
> and that everything, consequently, does not
> arrive in language but only comes to
> language. There is, therefore, no reason why

work and power should not be taken into
account in an anthropology of care where the
linguistic dimension finds its privileged,
yet subordinate place.[31]

Ricoeur would also acknowledge that a citique of
ideology can partially free itself from its initial
anchorage in preunderstanding historical hermeneutical
interpretation in the direction of the organized
knowledge that is the basis of a theory of institutions and phenomena of domination, the analysis of
reifications and alienations.[32] Ricoeur's argument
here provides a basis for assimilation of what is of
value in Habermas' concept of a communicative
rationality without having to contend that it stands
independently of an interpretation of a cultural heritage. This would embody the contention that a person
can be counted as rational who is able to interpret
his desires and feelings in light of culturally
established standards, but who is also able to take a
reflective attitude towards those standards and who is
able to learn from mistakes and free himself from
illusions.

In arguing this position, Habermas provides an
effective assimilation of Piaget's concept of the
decentration of egoistic understanding of the world as
a basis for comprehending what is involved in communicative rationality as the capacity for critical
reflection on what is given in the cultural background
of the lifeworld. While the lifeworld is a store of
interpretive work of previous generations, the more
there is a process of decentration, the more there is
a greater possibility of a critique of interpretations
stored in tradition.

Where Ricoeur wishes to challenge Habermas,
however, is on any separation of a critical social
sciences from the historical hermeneutical sciences.
Ricoeur believes it is necessary to be suspicious of
the old opposition between understanding vs. explanation that has been at the basis of this division. "If
the communication of past heritages takes place under
the conditions of distanciation and objectification,
then explanation is a necessary step for
understanding."[33] This can be illustrated in regard
to the systematic distortions that affect our competence to comminicate. It may be correct to say that
such distortions call for genetic explanations, but
this remains insignificant if not meant to reestablish
a competence to communicate which had deteriorated.

"My thesis here is that the interests in emancipation would be empty and anemic unless it received a concrete content from our practical interest in communication and, therefore, if it were not confirmed by our capacity to creatively reinterpret our cultural heritage."[34]

Ricoeur notes that Habermas, himself, recognizes that science and technology have become the dominant ideologies of the modern era, where a system of instrumental action replaced traditional forms of legitimation. A subsystem of instrumental action has overrun the sphere of communicative action, where the Greek ideal of the "good life" has been abolished in favor of the functions of a manipulated system. But if this is the case, Ricoeur contends, "how can the interest in emancipation remain anything more than a pious vow, save by embodying it in the reawakening of communicative action itself? And upon what will you concretely support the reawakening of communicative action, if not upon the creative renewal of a cultural heritage?" Habermas, in short, cannot deny that his interest in emancipation speaks out of a tradition; critique is also a tradition. "I would say that it plunges into the most impressive tradition, that of liberative acts, of the Exodus and the Resurrection."[35]

Ricoeur thus emphasizes that a creative appropriation of a cultural heritage, as the basis for an interest in emancipation, must derive from both Greek and Christian sources. Habermas, himself, recognizes the importance of the classical ideal of Aristotelian praxis as a focus upon normative questions of the good life, but he is convinced that the metaphysical aspects of this heritage are no longer credible in the modern age, as well as the fact that Aristotle's categories have been appropriated as a conservative defense of traditional practices.

But does the creative appropriation of the Aristotelian heritage require this judgment? Both Gadamer and Taylor, it has been seen, emphasize that the essence of Greek logos is not an outmoded correspondence theory of knowledge but a concept of human capacity for language as a basis for a common life in which men manifest to each other what is useful and harmful and, therefore, what is right and wrong. It was also noted that Gadamer's emphasis upon the concept of Aristotelian praxis as a model for hermeneutical interpretation is a recognition that understanding must be the application of universals to particular situations that require practical, prudential wisdom as opposed to theoretical technical knowledge. While the concept of Aristotelian praxis has been frequently involved by exponents of neoconservative ideologies, as Habermas contends, there is no intrinsic reason why it cannot provide a basis for critical reflection that serves legitimate interests in human emancipation and liberation.

Ricoeur's conviction that an interest in emancipation must embody a creative interpretation of a cultural heritage embodies central emphasis upon biblical themes of "freedom in light of hope," which will be considered in the concluding chapter. The critical theory of Habermas is part of a modern secular consciousness that would see religious world views as anachronistic and reactionary, as remnants of myth structures of traditional society that have been discredited by the learning process of human evolution. Yet, Habermas is cognizant of contemporary forms of political theology that are congenial to central themes of his critical theory. This is apparent from brief comments in his book <u>Legitimation Crisis</u> in which he speaks of the need for global integration to overcome historical contingencies in which world views have foundered on the separation of cognitive from socially integrative components.

Habermas points to constructive possibilities in repoliticizing of biblical interpretation in Jurgen Moltmann, Johannes Metz, Dorothee Soelle where the idea of God is the <u>logos</u> that determines the community of believers and life content of an emancipated society. God becomes the name for community structures that force men to go beyond accidental empirical nature to encounter another indirectly.[36] Habermas does not elaborate on this statement, but it is at least an indication he is not closed to the possible relevance of biblical heritage to the problem of liberation and emancipation in the modern era. How such a possibility has been articulated in the liberation theology of Gustavo Gutierrez will be the subject of the following chapter.

1. For the condensed summary of this background the author has relied heavily on Rick Roderick, Habermas and the Foundations of Critical Theory (New York: St. Martins Press, 1986), chap. 2.

2. Jurgen Habermas, Knowledge and Human Interests (Boston: Beacon Press, 1968), p. 42.

3. Ibid., p. 53.

4. Ibid., p. 55.

5. Ibid., p. 42.

6. Ibid., p. 196.

7. Ibid., p. 197.

8. Ibid., p. 308.

9. Ibid., p. 309.

10. Ibid., p. 310.

11. Jurgen Habermas, Theory and Practice (Boston: Beacon Press, 1974), p. 142.

12. Jurgen Habermas, Towards a Rational Society (Boston: Beacon Press, 1971), p. 96.

13. Ibid., pp. 62-80.

14. Habermas, Knowledge and Human Interests, p. 310.

15. Ibid., p. 314.

16. Richard Bernstein, "Introduction," Habermas and Modernity, edited by Richard Bernstein (Cambridge: MIT Press, 1985), p. 97.

17. Thomas McCarthy, The Critical Theory of Jurgen Habermas (Cambridge: MIT Press, 1978), pp. 91-125.

18. Jurgen Habermas, The Theory of Communicative Action, vol. I, Reason and the Rationalization of Society, translated by Thomas McCarthy (Boston: Beacon Press, 1981), pp. 1-3.

19.   Ibid., p. 10.

20.   Ibid., p. 16.

21.   Ibid., p. 100.

22.   Ibid., p. 19.

23.   Ibid., pp. 56-57.

24.   Ibid., pp. 69-70.

25.   Ibid., p. 71.

26.   Ibid.

27.   Ibid., p. 72.

28.   Roderick, p. 165.

29.   Paul Ricoeur, "Ethics and Culture," Political and Social Essays, collected and edited by David Steward and Joseph Bien (Athens: Ohio University Press, 1974),   p. 258.

30.   Ibid., p. 259.

31.   Ibid., p. 263.

32.   Paul Ricoeur, "Science and Ideology," in Paul Ricoeur Hermeneutics and the Human Sciences, edited and translated by John Thompson (London: Cambridge University Press, 1982), p. 244; "Hermeneutics and the Critique of Ideology," p. 11.

33.   Ricoeur, Political and Social Essays, p. 264.

34.   Ibid., p. 266.

35.   Ricoeur, "Hermeneutics and the Critique of Ideology," p. 99.

36.   Jurgen Habermas, Legitimation Crisis (Boston: Beacon Press, 1973), p. 121.

CHAPTER 5

GUSTAVO GUTIERREZ:
LATIN AMERICAN LIBERATION THEOLOGY

Latin American liberation theology has become one of the more dynamic and controversial intellectual forces of contemporary Latin American politics. Although identified with a minority left-wing perspective, liberation theology constitutes an important component within the larger context of progressive change in the political orientation of the Church in recent years. The chief inspiration for liberation theology stems from the Conference of Latin American Bishops at Medellin in 1968.[1] The central theme of the Medellin conference was that Latin America lives beneath a tragic sign of underdevelopment: hunger, misery, illness, infant mortality, inequalities of income; tension between classes and outbreaks of violence; the lack of participation of people in decisions affecting the common good; an external position of neocolonial dependency. The privileged classes, it alleges, are insensitive to the miseries of the marginal sectors and freequently resort to force to repress opposition with "anti-communism" or "keeping order" as the justification for their actions.[2]

Medellin presents an image of Latin American man living in a decisive moment of the historical process analogous to the Old Testament liberation of Israel from the oppression of Egypt, a passage from a condition of life that is less human to one that is more human, from oppressive social structures that come from the abuse of ownership and power and the exploitation of workers to a new society that will show respect for human dignity, the provision of basic necessities, and cooperation for the realization of a common good.[3]

The quest for justice is the central focus of Christian doctrine: it is God who sends his son to liberate men from slavery to which sin has subjected them, from the hunger, misery, oppression, and ignorance that has its origin in human selfishness. This will require a profound conversion, not so much in the demand for structural change but in the conversion of man who will in turn bring about such change. Love is the fundamental law of human perfection and the basis for the realization of justice in the world. This is not a question of confusing temporal progress with the Kingdom of Christ, but rather that the temporal order can contribute to a better ordering of human society that is of vital concern to the spiritual dimension. This means avoiding the dualism that separates the temporal from the spiritual, the recognition that Christian faith can be a force for liberating men from injustice and oppression, but also a concept of social justice as a concern for the whole life of man and an impulse towards the integral growth of our countries.[4]

The Church, through its pastoral activities, must seek to play a vital role in influencing the direction of social change. The church must denounce extreme inequalities between rich and poor and urge government and upper classes to limit the forces of injustice, inertia, venality, and insensibility.[5] Encouragement must be given to national communities as intermediate structures between the person and the state, where people have a means for creative participation in the construction of a new society.[6] In regard to business enterprise and the economy, the Medellin report takes a stand against both liberal capitalism and Marxism, both of which are seen as a violation of human dignity: the one based on profit making and the other concerned with collective man and the totalitarian concentration of state power. In influencing the direction of social change the Church must appeal to businessmen and political authorities to modify the goals and functions of business in terms of the social technings of Christ. Workers, who are in a situation of dependence that borders on physical, cultural, civil, and spiritual slavery, must be given the opportunity to participate in the running of industrial enterprises.[7]

While the theme of the Medellin conference is the liberation from oppression and social injustice, its proposals for social change (as should be evident from the previous discussion) are by no means revolutionary: Marxist doctrine is explicitly repudiated; social reform must be sought through the appeal to the moral conscience of the ruling classes rather than class struggle.[8] There is no identification of the Church with any specific political ideology or program. The use of violence as a political tactic is rejected. Medellin acknowledges that existing social structures of oppression and injustice are forms of institutionalized violence, and it concedes that the resort to violence as a means of combating prolonged tyranny may embody noble impulses. But armed revolution can only generate new forms of injustice and cause new disasters; one cannot combat evil at the price of a greater evil.[9]

Contemporary liberation theology, although emerging from the inspiration provided by the Medellin conference, moves in a more radical direction having some affinities with Marxist interpretation.[10] But the positions taken by liberation theologians are effectively argued within the framework of theological principles and the interpretation of biblical sources. There is, therefore, little foundation in the fears of the Church hierarchy, evident at the recent conference at Puebla, that liberation theology has become captive to Marxist ideology or that it has departed from the essential tenets of Christian faith. It can be argued, in fact, that liberation theology supplies what is lacking in positions taken at both the Medellin and the Puebla conferences: an effective articulation of the political basis of Christian faith in the context of Latin American historical realities.

The intention of this chapter is to defend this thesis by an examination of the contribution of Gustavo Gutierrez, one of the leading exponents of liberation theology. Gutierrez's contribution may be viewed in terms of four dimensions.

1. the meaning of liberation praxis as an outgrowth of contemporary developments in theology
2. his interpretation of the biblical meaning of human liberation
3. his appropriation of Marxist categories in the understanding of Latin American historical realities
4. his view of the role of the Church as a participant in the process of liberation

Liberation Praxis

The keynote theme of Gutierrez's political theology is the concept of historical praxis; and historical praxis, he contends, is liberation praxis, in identification with oppressed human beings and social classes and solidarity with their interests and struggles.[11] In viewing the theological foundations of this concept, Gutierrez speaks for a theology as a "critical reflection on praxis," which he sees in opposition to a classical theology as wisdom and rational knowledge. In the early centuries of the Church classical theology tended to be monastic, a

spiritual life removed from worldly concerns. Along
with this was the development of a theology of
Platonism and neo-Platonism as a metaphysics stressing
the transcendence of an absolute from which everything
came and to which everything returned. Present life
was regarded as contingent and of insufficient value.

From the twelfth century theology became a science
culminating in the thought of St. Thomas Aquinas, an
intellectual discipline seeking to achieve the
integration of faith and reason. Emerging out of this
was scholasticism, which, as a concern for systemati-
zation and clear exposition, became a degradation of
Thomism. After the Council of Trent the function of
scholastic theology, Gutierrez contends, became that
of defining revealed truth, denouncing and condemning
false doctrines, and teaching revealed truth authori-
tatively. Both spirituality and rational knowledge,
Gutierrez observes, are indispensable functions of all
theological thinking, but these functions must be
salvaged from the "divisions and deformations suffered
throughout history."[12]

The concept of theology as critical reflection,
Gutierrez believes, has been more clearly defined in
recent years, but its roots are in the first centuries
of the life of the Church. In the first place, the
concept of charity has been rediscovered as the center
of Christian life: St. Paul's concept that faith
works through love, where the understanding of truth
is not simply the affirmation of memorization of truth
but in commitment, attitude, and one's posture towards
life.

In a parallel development of the twelfth century
one finds the mixed life of contemplation and action
manifesting itself in recent years in the search for a
spirituality of laity and activity of the Christian in
the world. A further development is the greater sen-
sitivity to the anthropological aspects of revelation, the Word of God as a word about our situation
and relationships among men. This is not a horizon-
talism but a rediscovery of the indissoluble unity of
man and God. Vatican II has reaffirmed the Church of
service and not of power, the activity of the Church
in the world as a starting point, a theology of "signs
of the times" as a call to pastoral activity and the
commitment to service.[13]

Another factor of a philosophical nature is the
importance of human action as a point of departure for

all reflection in terms of the relations of man to nature and advances in science and technology. This includes the influence of Marxist analysis focusing upon the concept of praxis geared to the transformation of the world. Finally, there is the rediscovery of the eschatological dimension that has led to the reconsideration of the role of historical praxis. If human history is the opening to the future, then this requires a recognition of the political dimension through which man orients himself towards the gift that gives history its transcendent meaning; to "do the truth" acquires a precise meaning in terms of the actions of Christian life. The concepts of love and brotherhood are not foreign to the transformation of the world and it is only by "doing the truth" that faith is verified. Inherent in this is a concept of "orthopraxis" where the intention is to recognize the work and importance of concrete behavior and praxis in Christian life.[14]

These developments, Gutierrez believes, are thus a basis for the concept of theology as a critical reflection; theology follows, it is a second step; it must start from the facts and questions derived from the world and history. Theology, as such, does not replace other functions as wisdom and rational knowledge but these components must have ecclesial praxis as a point of departure and context.

> It is for these reasons that the theology of liberation offers us not so much a new theme for reflection as a new way to do theology. Theology as critical reflection on historical praxis is a liberating theology, a theology of the liberating transformation of the history of mankind and also therefore that part of mankind--gathered into ecclesia--which openly confesses Christ. This is a theology which does not stop with reflecting on the world, but rather tries to be part of the process through which the world is transformed. It is a theology which is open--in the struggle against the plunder of the vast majority of people in liberating love, and in the building of a new, just and fraternal society--to the gift of the Kingdom of God.[15]

Human Liberation

Gutierrez believes that the concept of liberation praxis has a basic grounding in the biblical themes of human salvation, God in history, eschatological hope and promise. The notion of salvation, Gutierrez contends, has changed from the past view as something otherworldly to which present life is merely a test. Salvation is rather something that embraces all human reality, transforming it and leading to fullness in Christ. This fulfillment embraces all aspects of life, body, and spirit--the individual and society. Sin is thus not only an impediment to salvation in an afterlife but a break from God; it is a historical reality and breach of communion of men with each other.[16]

The Bible establishes a link between creation and salvation, and this link is based on the historical and liberating experience of the Exodus. Biblical faith is a God who reveals himself through historical events, a God who saves in history. This vision is enriched by the liberation of Israel from Egypt, a liberation that is a form of political action, the breaking away from a situation of despoliation and misery and the beginning of the construction of a just and fraternal society. The Bible is a book of promise gradually revealed in all its universality and concrete expression; it is already fulfilled and concrete in historical events but not yet completely; it increasingly projects itself into the future creating a permanent historical mobility.[16] This is not only a spiritual redemption but a sense of fullness that takes on and transforms reality, and it is only in the temporal historical event that we can open up to the future of complete fulfillment.

> The prophets announce a kingdom of peace. But peace pre-supposes the establishment of justice, the defense of rights of the poor, punishment of the oppressors, social realities implying a historical liberation.[17]

Gutierrez believes that in Christ the all-comprehensiveness of the liberation process reaches its fullest sense. Sin is not considsered as an individual or merely interior reality; it is a social, historical fact, the absence of brotherhood and love in relationships among men. Sin is evident in the oppressive structures of exploitation of man by man in domination and slavery of people's races and social classes, the roots of situations of injustice and exploitation. Sin demands a radical liberation and that is the gift that Christ offers us, the liberation of men from all slavery to which sin has subjected them, the injustice and hatred that have their origin in human selfishness.[18]

A basic theme of the New Testament is a new ethic arising from the universal principle of love. This involves the concept of charity, not only in concrete actions of feeding the hungry and giving drink to the thirsty, but in the fabric of relationships among men. It is not an individual charity, but man considered in the fabric of social relationships and situated in his economic, social, and cultural coordinates. To offer food or drink in our day is a political action, the transformation of a society structured to the benefit of a few who appropriate to themselves the values of the work of others. This transformation will require a radical change in private ownership of the means of production.[19]

In emphasizing the political implications of the Gospels, liberation theologians are open to the criticism that they are engaging in an improper "politicizing" of the Gospels and that they are presenting a distorted picture of Christ as a political leader or crusader. But Gutierrez is well aware of the danger of this oversimplication. He recognizes that Christ kept his distance from the Zealot movement, which opposed the Roman Empire and which hoped to make Christ a king. The universality of his message did not conform to their narrow nationalism; oppression and injustice for Jesus was not limited to a specific historical situation. The causes go deeper and cannot be eliminated without going to the roots of the problem, the disintegration of brotherhood and communion among men. But there is a political implication in the fact that what he stood for brought him into confrontation with groups in positions of power, the Publicans and Sadducees whose official and privileged position was threatened; his criticism of religion based upon purely external laws and observances brought him into violent conflict with the Pharisees; his head-on opposition to the powerful and a radical option for the poor; and finally the fact that he "died at the hands of political authority."[20]

On the more positive side the universality of his message touches the very heart of political behavior. Misery and social injustice reveal a "sinful situation," a disintegration of brotherhood and communion. By freeing us from sin Jesus attacks the roots of an unjust order.

For Jesus, the liberation of the Jewish
people was only one aspect of a universal
permanent revolution. Far from showing no
interest in this liberation, Jesus rather
placed it on a deeper level with far reaching
consequences.

Although the concept of the Kingdom of God must not be
confused with the establishment of a just society, it
is not an indifference to that society.

The Kingdom of God is realized in a society
of brotherhood and justice; and in turn this
realization opens up the promise of hope and
complete communion of men with God. The
political is grafted into the eternal.[21]

In his stress upon the biblical theme of the promise of the future, Gutierrez attaches key importance
to the theology of hope indebted to both Ernst Bloch
and Jurgen Moltmann. For Bloch, man is he who hopes
and dreams for the future, but this is an active hope
that subverts the existing order, an acceptance of the
Marxist concept that philosophers have only
interpreted the world, the point, however, being to
change it. Hope is a "not-yet" consciousness,
assuming a concrete utopian function, mobilizing human
action in history. The ontology of what is "not yet"
is dynamic in contrast to the static ontology of
being, which is incapable of planning in history.[22]

Moltmann found in Bloch's analysis categories for
thinking through biblical themes of eschatology, promise, and hope. For Moltmann the biblical revelation
is not the Greek concept of the "epiphany of eternal
present," which limits itself to explaining what
exists. Revelation, on the contrary, is that which
speaks to us about a God who comes to meet us and for
whom we can only wait in active hope. Gutierrez
believes that Moltmann's concept of hope provides an
important contribution to contemporary theology. To
hope does not mean to know the future but to be open
to accepting it as a gift--a gift accepted in the
negation of injustice, in the protest against viola-
tions of human rights and the "struggle for peace and
brotherhood."[23]

In this emphasis upon the biblical concepts of
hope and promise for the future, Gutierrez seeks to
distinguish between a false versus authentic utopian
thought. A false utopianism is that which is irra-

tional and unreal. But a true utopian thinking, Gutierrez contends, is characterized by relationships to present historical realities. Utopian thought, he contends, embodies a dynamic element in the historical becoming of humanity. This occurs under two aspects: denunciation and annunciation. Utopian thought necessarily means a denunciation of an existing order that is dehumanizing and, for this reason, it is revolutionary rather than reformist.

But utopian thought is also an annunciation of what is not yet, the forecast of a different order of things, a new society, a field of creative imagination that proposes the alternative values to those rejected. In this respect it is a projection into the future, a dynamic and mobilizing factor in history. Between the denunciation and annunciation is the time for building a historical praxis. This is the meaning of utopia as a driving force of history; for if it does not lead to action in the present, it is an evasion of reality.

Utopian thought must be a commitment to creating a better society, otherwise denunciation remains at the verbal level and annunciation will only be an illusion. Utopian thought also belongs to the rational order; it emerges with renewed energy in times of transition and crisis when science has reached its limits as an explanation of social revolution and when new paths open up for historical praxis. In this respect utopian thought is neither opposed to nor outside of science. On the contrary, utopia provides a creative and dynamic factor as the prelude to science--its annunciation. It embodies theoretical constructs that imply creative imagination. This is the difference between utopian thought and ideology, for the latter does not offer adequate scientific knowledge of reality but masks it; it does not rise above the empirical, irrational level and functions in preserving the established order. Because of its relationship to reality, its implication for praxis, and its rational character, utopia is thus a factor of historical dynamism and radical transformation.

Gutierrez believes, finally, that the political, economic, and social aspects of liberation have a vital connection with faith, for faith and political action cannot enter into a correct and fruitful relationship except through the creation of a new type of person in a different society.

Utopia, so understood, far from making the
political struggler a dreamer, radicalizes
his commitment and helps him keep his work
from betraying his purpose--which is to
achieve a real encounter among men in the
midst of a free society without social
inequalities...the loss of utopia is responsible for man's falling into bureaucratism
and sectarianism, into new structures that
oppress men. The process, apart from
understandable ups and downs and deficiencies, is not liberating if the plan for a new
man in a freer society is not held to and
concretized. This plan is not for later,
when political liberation will have been
attained. It ought to go side by side with
the struggle for a more just society at all
times. Without this critical and rational
element of historical dynamism and creative
imagination, science and political action see
a changing reality slip out of their hands
and easily fall into dogmatism. And political dogmatism is as worthless as religious
dogmatism; both represent a step backward
towards ideology. But for utopia validly to
fulfill this role, it must be verified in
social praxis; it must become effective commitment, without intellectual purism, without
inordinate claims; it must be revised and
concretized constantly.[24]

Latin American Historical Realities

While Gutierrez's concept of liberation praxis is
firmly grounded in biblical-theological interpretation,
his analysis of Latin American historical realities
shows a clear appropriation of Marxist categories.
The central dynamic of Latin American oppression,
Gutierrez believes, stems from so-called developmental
policies designed to end foreign-oriented growth that
had made Latin American countries dependent exclusively on foreign trade. This was to be achieved by
means of an inward development involving import
substitution, expansion of internal markets, and
industrialization that would lead to independent
societies. This process was seen as one that would be
based on the model of developed societies, where the
archaic political structures of traditional or tran-
sitional societies would have to be overcome through
the cumulative effects of tension between opposing
forces. But developmentalism did not yield the

expected results and, after the decade of the 1960s, the gap between the developed and underdeveloped countries actually increased.

The fundamental error of the developmental theory was the failure to take into account political factors and the fact that; it remained with an abstract ahistorical framework. Emerging as a challenge to the developmental theory has been "dependency" theory, which contends that the underdevelopment of poor countries is the historical by-product of the development of other countries and that Latin America is in a situation of dependency upon the external domination of world markets that comprise the international capitalist system. The internal economies of Latin American countries have become more firmly bound to this structure; we are witnessing the "internalisation of the external market" and an "internalisation of dependence." While old forms of imperialist presence in terms of enclave economies still persist, we have a new type of dependency based on foreign investment in the modern sector of the economy, binding it more closely to international capitalism and the interests of multinational corporations.[25]

Gutierrez believes that a class analysis enables us to see what is really involved in the opposition between oppressed countries and dominant peoples. Reformist efforts have failed to realize that there can be an authentic development for Latin America only if there is a liberation from the domination exercised by the great capitalist countries, especially the United States. This means that the Latin American peoples will not emerge from their present status except by means of a social revolution that will radically and qualitatively change the conditions in which they now find themselves. Those leading the banner of Latin American liberation are most frequently of socialist inspiration, although this does not embody any monolithic orientation and there are many theoretical and practical diversities. But liberation means more than overcoming economic, social, and political dependency, for it embodies a deeper process of the emancipation of man in history where he will be free from servitude and the artisan of his own destiny. Gutierrez believes that one of the most creative efforts in this direction is the experimental work of Paulo Freire as a "pedagogy of the oppressed," a liberation as cultural action linking theory and praxis where the oppressed person modifies his relationship with the world and other people. This is a process Freire called "conscientisation" in which the oppressed person rejects the oppressive consciousness that dwells in him and finds his own language, where he becomes less dependent and freer as he commits himself to the transformation and building of society.[26]

The Church as Liberator

Gutierrez believes that the Church has an important role to play in the task of American liberation. In Latin America "to be Church" today means to take a clear position regarding the present state of social injustice and the revolutionary process that is the attempt to abolish this injustice and to build a more human order. This must entail the prophetic denunciation of the institutions that are contrary to brotherhood, justice, and liberty backed up by clear action and commitments. But this denunciation must also be the confronting of a given situation with the reality that is announced: the love of the Father, which calls all men to Christ and, through the action of the spirit, to union among themselves and communion with him. This means that the people who hear the message should perceive themselves as oppressed and feel impelled to seek their liberation.

Annunciation, therefore, has a conscienticizing function or, in other words, a political function in solidarity with exploited social classes. The preaching of the word, Gutierrez contends, will be empty and ahistorical if it tries to avoid this dimension. This is not a question of reducing the Gospel to the creation of a political consciousness among men, but that the annunciation of the Gospel as a message of total love has an inescapably political dimension as addressed to people living in social relationships that are dehumanizing.[27]

Gutierrez recognizes that the division into oppressed and oppressors and antagonistic classes in Latin America brings with it confrontation, struggle, and violence. The reality of class struggle poses problems to the universality of Christian love and the unity of the Church. But in Gutierrez's view any consideration of this subject must start from two elemental facts: that class struggle is a fact and that neutrality in this matter is impossible. Class struggle is a basic reality of social, political life independent of religious or ethical options; to ignore it is to deceive or to be deceived and to deprive oneself of the means of eliminating this condition and building a more free, humane, and just society. "To build a just society necessarily implies the actual and conscious participation in the class struggle that is occurring before our eyes.[28]

Second, to deny class struggle is to put oneself on the side of the dominant sectors. Neutrality is impossible. Gutierrez does not see this as being in conflict with the Gospel concept of love of all people. The universality of love, he contends, is only an abstraction unless it becomes concrete. To love all men does not mean avoiding confrontation or perceiving a fictitious harmony. Universal love is that which in solidarity with the oppressed seeks also to liberate the oppressors from their own power, ambition, and selfishness. In this sense the liberation of the poor and the rich are achieved simultaneously. One loves oppressors by liberating them from their inhuman qualities as oppressors. The Gospel injunction that one should love one's enemies, then, presupposes that one has class enemies and that it is necessary to combat them. "Love of enemies" does not ease consensus; rather it challenges the whole system and becomes a subversive formula.[29]

The face of class struggle challenges the unity of the Church and demands a redefinition of what this unity means. If the Church is in a world divided between antagonistic classes, then it cannot ignore that fact, and a religious attitude that tries to place itself beyond temporal contingencies falsifies the true character of the Christian community. In a radically divided world the function of the ecclesial community is to struggle against the causes of this division and this implies an option for the oppressed. In taking this action a unity will be forged not among those who say "Lord, Lord" but among those who "do the will of the Father." Thus the recognition of class struggle and participation in it will not be a negation of the message of unity but the discovery of the path by which the ecclesial community can free itself from what now prevents it from being a clear sign of brotherhood.[30]

The Church and Liberation Theology

Liberation theology, it has been seen, embodies radical implications that go considerably beyond the position articulated at the Medellin conference, and it is not surprising that it has been subject to strong attack from conservative Latin American bishops as well as the Roman curia and prominent West German theologians. This opposition was able to control the process of delegate selection to the conference at Puebla in 1979 so as to give tremendous edge to conservatives. Leading progressive bishops were conspicuous by their absence as well as leading Latin American liberation theologians.[31] It should be emphasized, however, that Puebla was not a repudiation of liberation theology and it embodies a continuity with Medellin as an indictment of the unjust, oppressive features of Latin American realities and the recognition that the Church must respond to the demands for justice and human liberation. But the Puebla conference also embodies a conservative reaction to particular themes associated with liberation theology. There is little in this critical reaction, however, that provides a convincing refutation of liberation theology and it only serves to indicate the powerful resistance within the Church hierarchy to any frank recognition of the political basis of Christian faith.

Although the Puebla document nowhere mounts a frontal attack upon liberation theology as a movement within the Church, it is sharply critical of what it refers to as a risk of "ideologisation" run by the theological reflection that has recourse to Marxist analysis. The consequence of this, it contends, is a total politicization of Christian existence, the "desacralisation" of the language of faith into that of the social sciences and the draining away of the transcendent dimension of Christian salvation.[32] But it is difficult to see how liberation theology can be faulted on this point. Gutierrez's concept of liberation praxis, it has been seen, is thoroughly grounded in contemporary theological developments as well as a biblical framework. The borrowing from Marxist analysis in regard to the understanding of Latin American historical realities springs from a valid contention that theological reflection upon historical praxis requires the assimilation of the secular sciences.

Other liberation theologians are supportive of Gutierrez's position on this point. Hugo Assman contends that purely theological criteria are not sufficient if drawn exclusively from the resources of theology. This is because such criteria are not clear in themselves and must be made to speak through the secular sciences, and because they are not related to present-day circumstances.[33] Luis Del Valle makes the same point in emphasizing that theology must be an empirical or inductive science, ascending fom the ground up, rather than a deductive science drawing conclusions from a priori principles.[34] Juan Scannone speaks of the role of social science in studying the material structures in which the "transcendent summons of the future is fleshed out," thus helping to differentiate truth from illusion.[35] The value of Marxism, Jose Bonino contends, is not in terms of a dogmatic materialism but what it provides as a way in which socioeconomic realities function at the level of history.[36]

The more serious charge against liberation theology is that its sympathy for Marxism entails taking an "ideological" position that is foreign to the authentic substance of Christian faith. If by ideology one means the adoption of disguises or rationalizations of narrow class interests or partisan perspectives as opposed to "truth claims" about human realities, this would be a valid criticism. But liberation theologians cannot be fairly accused of subscribing to ideological positions in this sense. Their contention is simply that Christian faith, as concern for the authentic meaning of social justice and human liberation, cannot escape the adoption of political-ideological positions. An ideological framework, as Jose Bonino contends, is always implicated in a given religious praxis. Every praxis articulates a view of reality and an ideology; there can be no neutrality. In the view of Juan Segundo, Christianity cannot avoid ideologies; God's revelation is never in a pure form; it is always fleshed out in historical ideologies.[37]

The Puebla document emphasizes that the Church must respect the pluralist character of Latin American society and it must not seek to impose a "catholic ideology."[38] But this cannot mean that the Church can claim neutrality from ideological positions. Puebla as well as Medellin emphasizes that the Church must take a position between the ideological positions of both liberal capitalism and Marxist collectivism. But this is no less an ideological position, one that was, in fact, given concrete political expression in the emergence of Christian Democratic parties in the period since World War I.

The basic issue then is not whether the Church should or should not become identified with a particular ideological position, but the problem of clarifying the nature of the ideological implication implied by the emphasis upon an alternative to liberal capitalism and Marxist collectivism as an approach to the goals of Latin American liberation. On a wide range of specific reforms liberation theology would be in full accord with positions taken at both Medellin and Puebla such as the role of the Church in denunciation of the social sources of poverty and in development of "conscientization" as to social, community problems.

1. the need for organizations among peasants and workers to defend their interests
2. the demand for social rights in regard to housing, education, and employment
3. the need for agrarian reforms

However, both Medellin and Puebla are essentially vague as to the political implications of liberation in regard to reconstruction of the economic order. Although clearly opposed to the structures of liberal capitalism, there is no endorsement of socialism as an objective. The Medellin document, it was previously noted, embodies only an appeal to business and political authority to modify the evaluation, the attitudes, and the means regarding the goals and functions of business in terms of the social teachings of the Church. But this embodies no implication that the basic structure of capitalism would be transformed. Its conviction that needed changes can be realized by appeal to the moral conscience of businessmen and political authorities displays a remarkable markable naivete about the realities of power and class interest that must be confronted in the task of social transformation.

Liberation theology, in contrast to both Medellin and Puebla, is the clear commitment to the necessity of a socialist alternative. This position stems from the simple but valid assumption that the subordination of the profit motive to a common good cannot be realized without a radical change in the private ownership of the means of production. Gutierrez believes this will mean taking the path of socialism, but a socialism that does not ignore the deficiencies of many of its actual historical undertakings, a socialism that tries to avoid cliches and prearranged schemes but creatively seeks its own path.[39]

Coupled with this is the contention that a state capitalism implied by the developmental model cannot be an adequate basis of Latin American liberation. It is possible, to be sure, that the developmental approach, as illustrated in such countries as Brazil or Mexico, may eventually vindicate the claims of its supporters that it can bring about material improvements for the lower classes parallel to the experience of European and American experience. However, present evidence is that the impressive rates of economic growth, especially in Brazil, have been exclusively to the benefit of an affluent middle class with continuing and even worsening poverty and misery for workers and the rural poor. The Cuban experience, by contrast, demonstrates that socialist planning is much more effective in providing for social justice and equality, both by comparison with prerevolutionary Cuba and with other Latin American countries. This does not mean that an authentic program of liberation must embrace a Marxist alternative but that some type of socialist planning will be necessary to overcome the inequalities that stem from the class divisions of Latin American society as well as the dependency upon an international capitalist system.

Perhaps the most controversial issue has to do with the question of revolutionary violence as a political tactic. Gutierrez's argument on this point, it was seen, is that class struggle is a basic reality of social political life. To deny this is to put oneself on the side of the dominant sectors. But Gutierrz does not see this in conflict with the Gospel concept of love; the love of all men does not mean avoiding confrontation and conflict; the Gospel injunction that one should love enemies presupposes that one has class enemies and that it is necessary to combat them. Gutierrez's argument on this point is obviously controversial, but it cannot be easily dismissed on the simple grounds that a Christian ethic requires a commitment to a doctrine of nonviolence and pacifism. Traditional Catholic social teachings, it is well to note, have always given place for the concept of a just war as well as the justifiable resistance to political tyranny.[40]

In regard to the just war theory Catholic doctrine seeks to establish criteria for determining the circumstances where the resort to armed force would be justifiable. This includes, for example, the assurance of having a just cause, the principle of proportionality or whether war can be considered a lesser evil than not using force, the principle that war should be only as a last resort after all other means have been exhausted.[41] These criteria are readily applicable to situations that have to do with revolutionary violence.

The real issue, then, is not a categorical choice between violence and nonviolence but the reasoned judgment that revolutionary force may be justifiable in a given situation where all other peaceful approaches have failed and where there is valid reason for believing that the good to be achieved by the use of force outweighs the evil it entails. Both the Medellin and Puebla statements embody a categorical condemnation of any form of political violence even in the face of prolonged tyranny on grounds that this only generates new injustices and evils. One cannot combat a real evil at the price of a greater evil.[42]

There is much to be said in favor of this position but not without recognition of possible exceptions. If one were to take seriously the Medellin and Puebla positions, then no legitimacy could be claimed for any of the major liberation movements of modern history including the Latin American independence movements and the American Revolution. In viewing contemporary revolutionary change in Latin America, the real question, then, is whether it is in fact true that the evils it has engendered have been greater than those it has intended to eradicate. It is difficult to see that the Cuban revolution (whatever its shortcomings) has generated worse evils than those that were part of the Batista regime it supplanted, and it can be seriously argued that Cuba is now one of the leading Latin American nations in regard to achievements in the direction of equality and social justice.

The revolution against the Somoza regime in Nicaragua is another case in point. The present failures, contradictions, and deficiencies of the Sandinista government are obvious enough. But it is certainly a reasonable contention that there have been at least relative gains in terms of liberation and social justice in comparison with the extreme inequalities and brutal police state terrorism of the Somoza regime.[43] It is also reasonable to argue that the present government will be able to make significant improvements in the future if a peace settlement is achieved.

The purpose of this chapter, in sum, has been to support the thesis that liberation theology, by contrast to the positions taken in both the Medellin and Puebla documents, provides a more effective articulation of the political basis of Christian faith and its relationship to the special problems posed by the nature of Latin American historical realities. It is, of course, not surprising that liberation theology represents only a minority position within the Church. Quite apart from theological considerations, the institutional Church encompasses a wide spectrum of social economic forces that it must seek to unify within the umbrella of the Catholic faith. To become identified with a particular faction would jeopardize this institutional unity.

It is encouraging, at least, that the Church positions as articulated at Medellin and Puebla have moved away from a traditional conservatism that has been in the past identified with the military and the landed oligarchy. The Medellin and Puebla statements, if not adequate to the construction of a political theology for Latin American liberation, provide a forthright diagnosis of Latin American realities and a sensitive realization that spiritual values must be given relevance to the quest for human dignity and social justice. It is not likely that the more radical orientation of liberation theology could have emerged without the inspiration provided by the conference at Medellin.

Liberation theology will continue to be a controversial left wing within the larger context of progressive change within the Church. But this should be seen as a source of creative tension and dialogue, and it is unfortunate that many members of the Church hierarchy view liberation theology as a seditious or subversive influence within the spectrum of Catholic faith.

1. Conference of Latin American Bishops (CELAM) 1970, _The Church in the Present-Day Transformation of Latin America in the Light of the Council_, Second General Council of Latin American Bishops, Division for Latin American Bishops, Division for Latin America, USCC, Washington, D.C., 1973.

2. Ibid., pp. 25, 55-57.

3. Ibid., p. 36.

4. Ibid., p. 43.

5. Ibid., p. 64.

6. Ibid., p. 43.

7. Ibid., p. 46.

8. Ibid., pp. 45-46.

9. Ibid., p. 63.

10. Gustavo Gutierrez is the leading exponent of this movement, best known to North American readers through his book, _A Theology of Liberation_, translated and edited by Sister Caridad Inda and John Eagleson (Maryknoll, N.Y.: Orbis Books, 1973). Other figures associated with this movement include Juan Luis Segundo, Hugo Assman, Raul Vidales, Jose Bonino, Jose Miranda, Juan Scannone. For a convenient anthology of articles by these writers see _Frontiers of Theology_, edited by Risino Gibellini, translated by John Drury (Maryknoll, N.Y.: Orbis Books, 1979).

11. Gustavo Gutierrez, "Liberation Praxis and Christian Faith," _Frontiers of Theology in Latin America_, edited by R. Gibellini (Maryknoll, N.Y.: Orbis Books, 1979), p. 24.

12. Gustavo Gutierrez, _A Theology of Liberation_ (Maryknoll, N.Y.: Orbis Books, 1973), p. 6.

13. Ibid., p. 8.

14. Ibid., p. 10.

15. Ibid., p. 15.

16. Ibid., p. 152.

17. Ibid., p. 167.

18. Ibid., p. 176.

19. Ibid., p. 202.

20. Ibid., pp. 225-229.

21. Ibid., p. 232.

22. Ibid., p. 216.

23. Ibid., p. 218.

24. Ibid., p. 237.

25. Ibid., p. 87.

26. Ibid., p. 91.

27. Ibid., p. 270.

28. Ibid., p. 274.

29. Ibid., p. 276.

30. Ibid., p. 278.

31. For a more detailed discussion of this opposition and the developments leading to Puebla see P. Lernoux, "The Long Path to Puebla," and M. Sancoval, "Report from the Conference," in Puebla and Beyond, edited by J. Eagleson and P. Sharper(Maryknoll, N.Y.: Orbis Books, 1979), pp. 3-43.

32. Eagleson and Sharper, p. 200.

33. H. Assman, Theology for a Nomad Church, translated by Paul Burns (Maryknoll, N.Y.: Orbis Books, 1976), p. 64.

34. R. Vidales, "Methodological Issues in Liberation Theology," in Gibellini, p. 40.

35. J. Scannone, "Theology, Popular Culture and Discernment," in Gibellini, p. 235.

36. J. Bonino, <u>Doing Theology in a Revolutionary</u> <u>Situation</u> (Philadelphia: Fortress Press, 1975), p. 97.

37. J. Segundo, <u>The Liberation of Theology</u> (Maryknoll, N.Y.: Orbis Books, 1976), p. 116.

38. Eagleson and Sharper, p. 273.

39. Gustavo Gutierrez, <u>Praxis of Liberation and</u> <u>Christian Faith</u> (San Antonio: Mexican American Cultural Center, 1976), p. 18.

40. M. T. Clark, ed., <u>An Aquinas Reader</u> (New York: Image Books, 1966), pp. 281-282.

41. For an excellent summary of Church teachings on this question see "The Challenge of Peace: God's Promise and Our Response, The Pastoral Letter of United States Bishops on War & Peace," <u>National</u> <u>Catholic Reporter</u>, June 17, 1983, pp. 11-15.

42. CELAM, p. 63.

43. For a detailed analysis that would lend support for this interpretation see "Nicaragua: A Fragile Future," <u>Sojourners</u>, March 1983, pp. 3-30. See also Gary MacEon, "Nicaragua: Can the U.S. Tolerate Moderation?" <u>Cross Currents</u>, Winter 1982-83, pp. 399-407.

CHAPTER 6

THE HERMENEUTICAL PHENOMENOLOGY OF PAUL RICOEUR
TOWARDS AN INTEGRATIVE PERSPECTIVE

Approaches to hermeneutical-praxis interpretations
considered in previous chapters reveal significant
variations and contrasts, particularly in the contrast
between the "hermeneutic of tradition" in Gadamer and
the "critique of ideology" in Habermas, and the
contrast between the philosophical hermeneutics of
Gadamer, Taylor, and Habermas as opposed to the
theological hermeneutic of Gutierrez. It would also
be apparent that the concept of liberation praxis and
its relationship to Marxist interpretation is a significant feature in the hermeneutical interpretations of
Habermas and Gutierrez that would not be shared by
Taylor, Gadamer, or Polanyi. But it has been the
intent of this study to emphasize the potentialities
for a unifying perspective as a possibility for truth
claims and normative universals in opposition to radical forms of "deconstructivism" represented by Rorty
and Foucault, and to contend that the belongingness to
a tradition is not incompatible with the interest in
liberation and emancipation in the terms emphasized by
Habermas and Gutierrez.

It is the purpose of this final chapter to argue
that the hermeneutical phenomenology of Paul Ricoeur
provides a hopeful prospect for an integrative
perspective at three key dimensions. One dimension is
his approach to ontological understanding that embraces Gadamer's emphasis upon the centrality of historical belonging but which also embodies a concept of the
"grafting of phenomenology unto hermeneutics" in order
to establish a critical "distanciation" within
historical belonging that is the basis for arbitration
between Gadamer's "hermeneutic of tradition" and
Habermas' "critique of ideology." A second dimension
of integrative perspective provided by Ricoeur is on
the relationship of faith to philosophical-ontological
understanding: his conviction that the unmasking of
false consciousness by a "hermeneutic of suspicion"
and "demythologizing" opens the way to an authentic
faith inspired by biblical symbols of hope and liberation and a philosophical approximation to biblical
kerygma in the Kantian concept of practical reason.
A third dimension of integrative perspective in
Ricoeur's political essays is an approach to problems

of social justice and liberation springing from a faith commitment he shares with Gutierrez but which also encompasses Gutierrez's dialogue with Marxism as well as the broader humanist heritage that animates the hermeneutical ontologies of Gadamer, Taylor, Habermas, and Polanyi.

I

The concept of hermeneutical interpretation, in terms best articulated by Gadamer, is the emphasis upon the centrality of texts, traditions, and social practices in opposition to the objectivist criteria of Enlightenment rationalism. While Ricoeur shares Gadamer's general commitment, he believes it is necessary to establish the basis for an ontology of understanding as the "grafting of hermeneutics onto phenomenology." Ricoeur sees this project as the end of a development running from Husserl to Heidegger. Ricoeur believes that it is necessary to give up the idea of a hermeneutics as a method to compete with natural science, which became entangled in the problem of subject vs. object distinction in the Kantian theory of knowledge.

> It is necessary to move outside of the problematic of subject vs. object and question oneself about being. But in order to question oneself about being in general, it is first necessary to question oneself about that being which is the "there" of all being, about <u>Dasein</u>, that is, about that being which exists in the mode of understanding being. Understanding is thus no longer a mode of knowledge but a mode of being, the mode of that being which exists through understanding.[1]

Ricoeur emphasizes both the value and limitation of Husserl's phenomenology in this endeavor. Husserl provided a necessary critique of the objectivist epistemology of the natural sciences as the only valid methodological model for the human sciences, and he contributed the concept of a "lifeworld" anterior to the subject-object relationship. The inadequacy of Husserl's phenomenology, however, is that his theory of meaning and intentionality involved Platonizing and idealist tendencies, the effort to reduce being to a "transcendental ego." A more adequate ontology of understanding, Ricoeur contends, must be more firmly grounded in a sense of historicity. The question of

100

historicity is no longer a response of human science to naturalistic explanation but a manner of being akin to being prior to encounter with particular beings. It is thus the historicity of being that becomes a constituting element of being.

Ricoeur believes that Heidegger contributes to an ontology of understanding no longer as a mode of knowledge but a mode of being. Yet, Ricoeur believes it is necessary to join phenomenology to hermeneutics in a way different from that of Heidegger. For Heidegger, in Ricoeur's view, does not provide a clear comprehension of how historical science can be founded in face of the challenge of the natural sciences. He wants to subordinate historical knowledge to ontology without showing in what sense historical understanding can be derived from this primordial understanding. Ricoeur believes that, in contrast to the "short route" taken by Heidegger's ontology of understanding, it is necessary to take the "long route" that begins by the analysis of language. It is always in language that ontological understanding arrives at its expression. "It is thus not vain to look to semantics for an axis of reference for the whole of the hermeneutical field."[2]

It should be emphasized that Ricoeur is not opposing a hermeneutical interpretation against phenomenology, as such, but only against its idealist version in Husserl. But Ricoeur believes that hermeneutical interpretation requires a phenomenological presupposition.

> The most fundamental phenomenological presupposition of interpretation is that every question concerning any sort of being is a question about the meaning of that being and, as such, the phenomenological attitude is already placed above the naturalistic-objectivist attitude. The choice in favor of meaning is thus the most general presupposition of any hermeneutics.[3]

Hermeneutics also comes back to phenomenology in the concept of "distanciation" at the heart of the experience of belonging as a distancing from "lived experience" as purely and simply adhered to. A linguistic sign, for example, can stand for something only if it is not that thing; where a sign possesses a specific negativity. Hermeneutics must thus incorporate a critical movement or suspicion that can be related to belonging only if distanciation is "consubstantial" with belonging. "Phenomenology shows that this is possible when it elevates to a philosophical decision the virtual act of instituting the empty space which enables a subject to signify his lived experience and his belonging to a historical tradition."[4]

Ricoeur also cites Gadamer's emphasis upon the concept of "play" as noted in Chapter 1, which doubtlessly summons the linguistic medium but which, in principle, antecedes and supports it. Ricoeur thus believes that the reference of the linguistic order back to the structure of experience constitutes an important phenomenological presupposition of hermeneutics.

But Ricoeur is in full agreement with Gadamer that distanciation cannot finally be seen in independence from the ontological conditions of belonging and being in the world that precedes reflection, and the concept of the interpretive process by which, in the interplay of question and answer, interlocutors collectively determine contextual values that structure their conversation. This would emphasize that the concept of distanciation cannot be separated from the ontological priority of belonging to a historical tradition and the mediation by the text as writing, documents, and monuments connected with the transmission of a historical tradition. This common feature of the text is the meaning contained therein that is independent of the intentions of the author, inviting a multiplicity of meaning and readings. Such a concept of the understanding of interpretation is thus opposed to any project of "ultimate foundation." "We arrive, as it were, in the middle of a conversation in which we try to orient ourselves in order to contribute to it." In Ricoeur's view this move puts into doubt any ultimate foundation as a phenomenological idealism. "The essential question is not to recover a lost intent but to unfold in front of the text a world which it opens up and discloses."[5]

Ricoeur's concept of distanciation at the heart of the experience of belonging becomes the basis for overcoming the conflict between a "hermeneutic of tradition" vs. a "critique of ideology." It is Ricoeur's conviction that while the two theories speak from a different place, it is possible that each can recognize the other's claim to universality in a way that marks the place of one in the structure of the

other. But this requires that overcoming the dichotomy of "explanation vs. understanding" associated
with difference between the natural and human science.

If the communication of a past heritage takes
place under conditions of distanciation and objec-
tivity, then explanation is a necessary step for
understanding. A text must be explained in its internal structure before being understood in terms of the
interest it arouses and to which it responds. The
same is true for ideologies that distort the capacity
to communicate. It would be correct to say that such
distortion derives from genetic explanation, but this
makes no sense if it does not reestablish a larger
field of consciousness and the restoration of the competence to communication that has been distorted.

Another way the hermeneutic of the text turns
toward a critique of ideology is in terms of the world
opened up by it. This implies a dimension of reality
against any given reality, a process that is well
illustrated in the subversive power of poetic
discourse. Such discourse involves the suspension of
the reference of ordinary language and releases a
second order of reference as a world opened up by the
work. "Thus, a distanciation emerges at the heart of
references: poetic discourse distances itself from
everyday reality, aiming at being as power to be."[6]

Ricoeur also acknowledges a concept of distanciation as a critique of ideology that can partially
free itself from its initial anchorage in preunderstanding towards a type of knowledge as the theoretical analysis of institutional reifications and
alienations, the role of critical social science as
the effort to unmask ideological frozen relation of
dependence that can be transformed through such critique. What Ricoeur insists upon, however, is that such
knowledge is partial and fragmentary and that it is
"hermeneutically founded on an original and unsur-
passable condition that makes distanciation a movement
of belonging."[7]

Ricoeur thus challenges the contention of Habermas
that an interest in emancipation is distinct from the
historical hermeneutical sciences. The interest in
emancipation, he contends, would be quite empty and
abstract if it were not situated on the plane of communicative action. "The task of the hermeneutic of
tradition is to remind the critique of ideology that
man can project his emancipation and anticipate an

unlimited and unrestrained communication only on the basis of the creative reinterpretation of a cultural heritage."[8]

Ricoeur notes that Habermas, himself, recognizes that science and technology have become the dominant ideologies of the modern era where a system of instrumental action replaced traditional forms of legitimation. A subsystem of instrumental action has overrun the sphere of communicative action where the Greek ideal of the "good life" has been abolished in favor of the functions of a manipulated system. But if this is the case, Ricoeur contends, how can the interest in emancipation remain anything more than a pious view if it does not awaken an interest in emancipation? "And upon what will you concretely support the reawakening of communicative action, if not upon the creative renewal of a cultural heritage?" Habermas, in short, cannot deny that his interest in emancipation speaks out of a tradition; critique is also a tradition. "I would say that it plunges into the most impressive tradition that of liberative acts, of the Exodus and the Resurrection."[9]

II

A second dimension on which Ricoeur provides an integrative focus is in regard to the relationship of faith to philosophical-ontological reflection. In understanding Ricoeur's approach to this relationship, it is important, first of all, to emphasize what he sees to be the preliminary role of a "hermeneutic of suspicion." Ricoeur warns against the danger of forms of mystification and false consciousness that have infected modern culture. It is for this reason that a critique of religion requires the assimilation of the impact of three masters of suspicion: Marx, Nietzsche, and Freud. The fundamental contribution of Marx does not remain his theory of class struggle but the discernment of the hidden relation that connects ideology to the phenomena of domination. What is of significance in Marx is neither his science nor that he is a moralist but his view of capitalism as a creation of false values and the history of the great "money fetish." The contribution of Nietzsche is a certain "hermeneutic of the will" in its significations and projections of values. The significance of Freud is what he reveals as a geneology of desire, his critique of religion as a compensation stemming from fear or as a substitute for prohibited pleasures.[10]

Among these writers there is also a common affirmation as well as a suspicion, the concern for restoring man's positivity. In Marx this embodies the mastery of alienating forces and the "leap from necessity to freedom." In Nietzsche, since God is dead in a cultural sense, there must be a new birth of man, which can be anticipated through the broken myths of the "superman," the "Eternal Return," and "Dionysus," triple myths of the future and of the will to power. In Freud there is the problem of passing from the pleasure principle to the reality principle, the struggle between Eros and death, the life and death instincts. A critique of religion nourished by these writers, Ricoeur contends, pertains to the mature faith of modern man. "A Marxist critique of ideology, Nietzsche's critique of resentment and the Freudian critique of infantile distress are views through which any kind of mediation of faith must pass."[11]

Ricoeur extends the external critique of religion to an internal critique of demythologizing associated with Rudolf Bultmann. This would focus upon the estrangement of the discourse of our cultural world and the cultural world of the Gospel. The preaching of the Gospel is a "folly for the world," a preaching not rooted in our experience, an eruption of something from the other side into our culture. But the kerygma has become a fact of our culture, creating new works and affirmations.

There is thus a double relation of discontinuity and continuity. As discontinuity it remains a "folly for the intelligent and a scandal for the wise." But at the same time (in the contributions of Bultmann and Barth), a new structure of communication has appeared. The eschatological world view of heaven and hell was not a scandal for ancient man. "It has become a scandal for modern man, but this scandal is not that of the cross, but the false scandal of a cultural vehicle that is no longer ours." Herein lies the legitimacy of Bultmann's "demythologizing," to disassociate the true scandal from the false scandal in order to have the true scandal, the original scandal revealed to all.[12]

Ricoeur is thus convinced that beyond the critical reflection that must unmask false consciousness, it is possible to salvage an authentic faith that is inspired by symbolic meaning. Ricoeur believes symbols have a triple root, "a basically psychic root--of desire, of the libido as Freud said--and, therefore, in the archeology of human desire which comes to the surface in oneric language; a cosmic root by its liaison to appearances (or apparitions) of the universe; and finally it is born in the relation of image to language in the world of the poet."[13] It is the responsibility of the philosopher to show that symbolism is not a deficient language.

In his book The Symbolism of Evil, Ricoeur seeks to show that symbolic language, as an indirect approach to the confession of evil in religious consciousness, lies within the sphere of philosophy, for it is an utterance of man about himself that must be taken up into philosophical discourse. Behind all speculation, however, we find myths as a narrative that relates events that happen in the beginning of time and that provide grounds for ritual actions of men--the forms of action and thought by which man understands himself and the world.

But myths have a symbolical function in discerning and revealing the bond between man and what he considers sacred. Speculation on original sin, Ricoeur believes, sends us back to the myth of the fall and the confession of sin. Implicit in this mythical language is an already symbolical language: defilement is spoken of under the symbols of "stain" or "blemish." Symbols are signs that aim at something beyond themselves, but not every sign is a symbol. Characteristic of symbols, Ricoeur believes, is a double intentionality. The literal meaning of defilement is "stain," but upon this first intentionality there is erected a second intentionality, which through the physically "unclean" points to a certain situation of man in the sacred, which is precisely that of being defiled, impure. The literal manifest sense points beyond itself to something that is _like_ a stain or spot. "Symbolic signs are opaque, because the first literal obvious meaning points analogically to a second meaning that is not given otherwise in it.... This opacity constitutes the depth of symbol, which is inexhaustible."[14]

A central component of symbolism, Ricoeur contends, is a poetic imagination. In his Essays on Biblical Interpretation, Ricoeur rejects a classical onto-theology or proofs of God in favor of a discourse close to experience as traits of truth capable of being spoken in terms of "manifestation" rather than verification, a manifestation of the world by text and scripture. What is involved in this process of

interpretation, he believes, is the revelatory function of poetic discourse. Poetic language restores us
that participation--in or belonging--to an order of
things that precedes our capacity to oppose ourselves
to things taken as objects opposed to subjects.

> Hence the function of poetic discourse is to
> bring about this emergence of a depth struc-
> ture of belonging amidst the ruins of
> descriptive discourse. Here truth no longer
> means verification but manifestation, i.e.,
> letting what shows itself be. What shows
> itself is in each instance a proposed world,
> a world I may inhabit and wherein I can pro-
> ject my ownmost possibilities. It is in this
> sense of manifestation that language in its
> poetic function is a vehicle of revelation.[15]

Ricoeur contends that symbolical meaning must be
regarded as a presupposition of philosophical reflection. Symbols, he contends, are not alien to philosophical discourse but are already an element of
speech. A mediation of symbols starts from speech
that has already taken place in some fashion.
"Wherever a man dreams or raves, another man arises to
give an interpretation; what was already discourse,
even if incoherent, is brought into coherent discourse
by hermeneutics."[16] This does not mean that we go
back to a "primitive naivete" but rather aiming at a
"second naivete" in and through criticism. "In short,
it is by interpretating that we can hear again."[17]
This involves a hermeneutical circle: "We must
understand in order to believe, but we must believe to
understand." We go beyond the circle of hermeneutics
by a wager.

> I wager that I will have a better
> understanding of man if I follow the indica-
> tions of symbolic thought. That wager then
> becomes the task of verifying my wager and
> saturating it, so to speak, with intelligi-
> bility. In return, the task transforms my
> wager: in betting on the significance of the
> symbolic world, I bet at the same time that
> my wager will be restored to me in the power
> of reflection, in the element of coherent
> discourse.[18]

In his discussion of biblical interpretation
Ricoeur speaks of a philosophical discourse that puts
itself into proximation with kerygmatic theological

discourse. "A work of thought is a work that begins by listening, and yet within the autonomy of responsible thought. It is an incessant form of thinking but within the limits of reasons alone."[19] Ricoeur believes that we must start from the Gospel Kerygma of freedom that, in his view, Jurgen Moltmann has most effectively articulated in his book The Theology of Hope: the central preaching of the resurrection interpreted as a theology of hope and promise of the future--the "already" of resurrection that orients us to the "not yet" of final recapitulation. The linkage of freedom to hope entails an "ethics of mission" that has communitarian, political, and cosmic implications that existentialist decision, centered on the personal, tends to hide. "A freedom open to new creation is in fact less centered on subjectivity, on personal authority, than on social and political justice; it calls for a reconciliation which itself demands to be inscribed in the recapitulation of all things."[20]

What is the approximation in the philosophical discourse in the kerygma of hope? The exegesis of hope by means of freedom is already a way of thinking according to the hope. We cannot remain in nondialectical opposition between promise and Greek logos; I hope in order to understand. In Ricoeur's view the discourse of the philosopher on freedom is discourse on "religion within the limits of reason alone," or what he characterizes as a "post Hegelian-Kantianism."[21]

What is of value in Hegel is the concept of morality as part of a larger trajectory of the realization of freedom, a philosophy of will that moves from abstract right to the spheres of objective and concrete morality in family, economic, and political community. The problem of Hegel, however, is the discordance between a speculative philosophy and human actuality, a philosophy that comes "too late to preach what the world ought to be like."[22]

Kant surpasses Hegel as a philosophy of limits rather than a philosophy of system. This would emphasize the function of the horizons of reason in the construction of knowledge and will, a philosophy of limits that is at the same time a practical demand, what Ricoeur sees to be the best philosophical response to "freedom in light of hope." This starts from the "thought of the unconditioned" and thought by way of objects. In hope I necessarily deceive myself by forming absolute objects: self, freedom, and God.[23]

The dialectic of practical reason, as a second step, is essentially a transposition to the will of the complete structure of pure reason where the concept of the highest good is purified of all speculation and measured by the problematic of practical reason, that is of the will. Here we have no longer a theoretical but a practical illusion, a subtle hedonism that introduces an interest into morality under the pretense of happiness. Thus, the religious meaning of beatitude (reward, consolation, etc.) is approached philosophically by the idea of a nonanalytic liaison between the work of man and the contentment susceptible of satisfying the desire that constitutes human existence. But for the philosopher this liaison is not meaningless. He can even say that it is a priori (morally) necessary to bring forth the highest good through the freedom of the will. It is a rational approximation to hope, residing in what is demanded and expected between morality and happiness.[24]

A third approach to hope is in terms of religion itself but "religion within the limits of reason alone" by means of the postulates of freedom, immortality, and the existence of God. The postulate of freedom is the perfect willing of a rational being; a freedom that is not a theoretical abstraction but has an objective reality and crowns the concept of persons taken as an end. The concept of immortality is an aspect of our need to effectuate the highest good in reality, expresses the force of hope of the postulate of freedom, the philosophical equivalent of the "hope for resurrection." It is this movement that enables us to pass from ethics to religion. The postulate of the existence of God is the manifestation to our will of the highest good, a nexus between the practical and religious, obligation and belief, moral necessity and existential hypothesis. The transcendent synthesis of the highest good, Ricoeur believes, is the closest philosophical approximation to the kingdom of God according to the Gospels. "Moral philosophy engenders philosophy of religion where hope of fulfillment is added to the consciousness of obligation."[25]

Finally, the Kantian concept of "religion within the limits of reason alone" converges with kerygma in the recognition that freedom holds the propensity for evil. "The 'postulate' of freedom must cross through not only the night of knowing, with its crisis of the transcendental illusion, but also the night of power with its crisis of radical evil. "Real freedom can spring up only as hope beyond this speculative and practical Good Friday. Nowhere are we close to the Christian kerygma: hope is hope of resurrection, resurrection from the dead."[26]

The doctrine of radical evil, Ricoeur believes, furnishes a receptive structure for forces of alienation at the level of culture as church and state, where falsified expressions take place, where true religion is in debate with false religion, and where the regeneration of freedom is liberated from the idols of the marketplace.

> This whole process constitutes the philosophy of religion within the limits of reason alone; it is this process which constitutes the philosophical analogue of the kerygma of the Resurrection. It is also this process which constitutes the whole adventure of freedom and which permits us to give comprehensible meaning to the expression "religious freedom."[27]

This singular merit of Ricoeur's hermeneutical interpretation, in conclusion, is the demand it makes upon us to dwell with the tension between reason and faith in spite of the futility of hope for absolute knowledge or certitude. Ricoeur expresses his accord with Barth that the origin of faith is the solicitude of man by the object of faith; to believe is to listen to the call, but to hear the call we must interpret the message; we must believe in order to understand and understand in order to believe.

> I will say, then that this circle can only be broken by the believer in the hermeneutic when he is faithful to the community, and by the hermeneutic in the believer when he does his scientific work of exegesis. This is the dual condition of modern man in whom struggles both a believer and an atheist; in the believer himself there confront one-another an adult critic and a naive child who listens to the Word.[28]

III

Ricoeur provides a final area of integrative focus that encompasses the integrity of both Christian and humanist sources in regard to issues of social justice

and human liberation. Here Ricoeur shares with
Gutierrez the general conviction that Christian love
must be a liberation praxis in identification with the
underprivileged and oppressed. This is not to say
that Ricoeur's definition of liberation praxis would
be wholly identical with that of Gutierrez. It was
seen in the previous chapter that Gutierrez speaks out
of conditions peculiar to the Latin American
situation: the poverty and oppression that result
from class domination and external economic exploitation. It is for this reason that Gutierrez, while
rejecting a doctrinaire Marxist materialism, sees the
relevance of conventional Marxist categories of class
struggle analysis in viewing the Latin American
situation.

But Ricoeur (just as Habermas) is closer to the
main thrust of European revisionist Marxism that has
been less concerned with the problem of poverty and
class domination and more with the question of
bureaucracy and technological domination in advanced
industrial societies. Yet Ricoeur is sensitive to the
problems that concern Gutierrez, and he recognizes
that the concept of Christian love must be directed to
problems of inequalities in the distribution of wealth
between "have and have not" nations and the measures
that will be needed to achieve a better distribution
of wealth.[29] Ricoeur's political analysis thus provides a framework that can assimilate the concerns of
liberation theology as a focus upon special problems
of Third World underdevelopment but which also
confront problems that are more crucial in the task of
socioeconomic transformations in postindustrial
societies that go beyond issues of economic inequalities and poverty.

Ricoeur subscribes to the goals and aims of a
democratic socialism that would be a response to human
needs at several key dimensions. At the economic
level this must involve economic planning in terms of
a criterion of economic rationality taking into
account human needs and the collective appropriation
of the means of production. At the political level it
would mean the effort to foster the realization of
democracy in industry that can avoid the danger of a
new slavery through bureaucratic domination. At the
cultural level a socialist humanism must address the
oldest theme of socialist vision in regard to the
alienation of work and the emphasis upon human responsibility over blind mechanisms in politics, administration, and bureaucracy. "Overcoming these

dangers means going back to what is closest to the heart of socialism as the cry of the distressed, the demand of the most humbled men."[30]

While Ricoeur's approach to political ethics is obviously animated by the biblical concept of "freedom in light of hope," as previously noted, it was also seen that he emphasizes a philosophical approximation to the biblical kerygma in the Kantian concept of practical reason. It is here that Ricoeur's hermeneutical phenomenology becomes a framework that is able to respect the contribution of both humanist and Christian sources. Ricoeur sees a true and authentic humanism as part of a Greco-Latin heritage as the "resistance to forgetfulness." This is justified by the function of memory that is the heart of culture, which makes it unnecessary to surrender oneself to the tide of contradictory influences of modern world. "It is not possible to conserve an original cultural personality without a living tradition."[31]

Humanism, Ricoeur contends, appears as the only reply to the objectification of man in work and consumption, the function of every disinterested cultural activity is the struggle against objectification through reflection and mediation. In terms very much similar to Habermas, Ricoeur protests against the objectifying features of a technology of behavior (such as that of B. F. Skinner). Ethical and political issues require a theory of action that can bypass the alternatives of "mentalism vs. behaviorism." Ricoeur believes this theory has been well articulated in linguistic analysis of Wittgenstein, Taylor, and Austin as an emphasis upon both the distinctive subtlety and coherence of ordinary language and its repudiation of the dualisms of interior and exterior. This does not require choosing between a "wild freedom" vs. a technology of behavior but rather an emphasis upon the relation of freedom and institutions. This presupposes that man may designate his action as his intentions, justify them by the reasons for which he claims to perform them, and ascribe them to himself as the agent of his own doing. The concept of institution covers all kinds of social bodies in which the individual plays roles in accordance with rules that prescribe behavior that contributes to the functioning of the whole body. From this standpoint a concept of the technology of behavior, Ricoeur believes, is too univocal; it cannot cover the field of freedom and institutions. The philosophical task is not to deny the concept and the promise of technology but to locate it within a larger framework.

Ricoeur believes that the concept of an autonomous man against which Skinner argues, needs to be clarified in the context of a Kantian approach to the problem of freedom. Autonomy is not something that exists but a task to be achieved. Second, we owe to Kant the concept of freedom as a practical concept, because the kind of law to which it is linked is not a law in the sense of a law of nature but a nonempirical law, an obligation. Third, there is no ethical or political problem, if we do not take into account the principle of mutuality from person to person, the recognition of another freedom, the position of the other as having as much value as I have.

> Here is the fundamental limit of a technology of behavior since it cannot take into account the notion of a person as "as an end in itself" which is constitutive of the concept of human dignity.... Freedom is no longer an extension of my attempt to escape control or avoid constraint. It is the extension of my recognition of the equal right of the other to exist.[32]

Thus the problem of freedom and of institutions has to be built on the basis of practical, normative, and intersubjective concepts such as those that Kant established.

Ricoeur's concept of humanism as an appropriation of Kantian categories, converges with humanist features of other representatives of hermeneutical interpretation that have been considered in this study. Gadamer's hermeneutical theory, it was seen involves the contention that it is by virtue of human language that there exists in man common meaning and a common life in which moral judgments or right and wrong are possible. Taylor, in similar terms, contends that language is a "being in the world" including the whole gamut of symbolic expressions having to do with subject-referring emotions of dignity, guilt, moral obligation. In the view of Polanyi the democratic ideals of truth, justice, and freedom are the premises of all forms of personal knowing. Habermas' concept of communicative rationality involves the defense of the possibility of intersubjective recognition of validity claims of truth, rightness, sincerity, and comprehensibility.

What becomes most controversial in concept of a hermeneutical ontology is, of course, most apparent in

these formulations. From the standpoint of
"deconstructivist" critics, they are all examples of
mistakes philosophers have always made in an attempt
to establish permanent foundations or basic
constraints. In considering this question at various
points in previous chapters, it has been the attempt
to argue that the above representatives of hermeneutical interpretations constitute a constructive
move in a direction beyond philosophical absolutism
vs. historical relativism. But it has not been the
intent to argue that such a position can be defended
in terms of any dogmatic finality.

An obvious objection to Ricoeur's hermeneutical
ontology, from the standpoint of deconstructivist critics, would be that Ricoeur's recourse to the Kantian
concept of practical reason as a philosophical
approximation to biblical kerygma of hope and liberation is falling back on the very foundationalism that
a hermeneutical interpretation is supposedly intended
to avoid: the concept of an ahistorical autonomous
rationality that can establish a basis for normative
principles. But this criticism would be to miss the
force of Ricoeur's contention that hermeneutical
interpretation, while the denial of any claims to
absolute knowledge, must sustain an "ontological hope"
at the limits of knowledge. A philosophy of limits,
Ricoeur contends, belongs both in the Christian and
Kantian strain of thought. The Christian concept of
the Last Judgment in regard to the totality of history
is always to shatter the pretensions of absolute
knowledge.

The Christian eschatology as the emphasis upon the
openness of history, joins with the limit idea in the
Kantian sense. "I think everything and I demand
everything but I am unable to know it." This must be
the fundamental principle of the thesis according to
which the efficaciousness of the man of culture and
its corollary in liberal politics of culture is the
object of belief and not of knowledge.

> Why still call this philosophy of limits a
> humanism? Because the word <u>human</u> in humanism
> sums up all its meaning. Man is a man when
> he knows that he is <u>only</u> man. The ancients
> called man a "mortal." This remembrance of
> death indicated in the very name of man
> introduces the reference to a limit at the
> very heart of the affirmation of man himself.
> When faced with the pretensions of absolute

114

knowledge, humanism is, therefore, the indication of an "only," we are only men. No
longer "human, all too human": this formula
still shares the intoxication of absolute
knowledge; but "only human." This formula
protects the sobriety of humanism.[33]

Ricoeur recognizes that ontological understanding
cannot be separated from interpretation and for this
reason it is not triumphjant; it cannot escape the
warfare of rival interpretations. But in spite of
this precariousness it is possible to contend that
rival hermeneutics are not mere "language games."

    In his appropriation of Kantian categories Ricoeur
emphasizes the quest for truth as a "regulative idea"
with the task of imposing unity on the diversity of
our field of knowledge. Truth constitutes the horizon
of my intended goals. For Ricoeur, just as for
Polanyi, the search for truth stretches between two
poles. At one pole there is the personal situation of
a certain interest with respect to being, something to
discover personally, a place to raise questions that
are unique to the situation. But at the other pole
the search for truth is an aspiration to something
that stands out in the background of my situation as
something that is universal. The search for truth,
Ricoeur contends, is itself "torn between the finitude
of my question and the openness of being." Inherent
in this process is an ontology of hope. "I hope that
I am within the boundaries of truth." This hope does
not give us power to master history or to order it
rationally.[34] "In this way ontology is indeed the
promised land for a philosophy that begins with
language and with reflection; but like Moses, the
speaking and reflecting subject can only glimpse this
land before dying."[35]

1. Paul Ricoeur, "Existence and Hermeneutics," in _Hermeneutical Inquiry_, vol. II, _The Interpretation of Existence_, edited by David E. Klemm (Atlanta, Ga.: Scholars Press, 1986), p. 188.

2. Ibid., p. 190.

3. Paul Ricoeur, "Phenomenology and Hermeneutics," in _Paul Ricoeur Hermeneutics and the Human Sciences_, edited and translated by John B. Thompson (London: Cambridge University Press, 1985), p. 114.

4. Ibid., p. 117.

5. Ibid., p. 111.

6. Ibid., p. 94.

7. Ibid., p. 244.

8. Ibid., p. 97.

9. Ibid., p. 100.

10. Paul Ricoeur, "The Critique of Religion," in _The Philosophy of Paul Ricoeur_, edited by Charles E. Reagan and David Stewart (Boston: Beacon Press, 1978), p. 217.

11. Ibid., p. 219.

12. Ibid., p. 221.

13. Paul Ricoeur, "The Language of Faith," in Reagan and Stewart, p. 233.

14. Paul Ricoeur, _The Symbolism of Evil_ (Boston: Beacon Press, 1969), p. 15.

15. Paul Ricoeur, _Essays on Biblical Interpretation_ (Philadelphia: Fortress Press, 1979), p. 102

16. Ricoeur, _Symbolism_, p. 350.

17. Ibid., p. 351.

18.   Ibid., p. 355.

19.   Ricoeur, <u>Essays on Biblical Interpretation</u>, p. 156.

20.   Ibid., p. 162.

21.   Ibid., p. 167.

22.   Ibid., p. 69.

23.   Ibid.

24.   Ibid., p. 172.

25.   Ibid., p. 177.

26.   Ibid., p. 179.

27.   Ibid., p. 180.

28.   "Ricoeur, Religion and Faith," in <u>The Philosophy of Paul Ricoeur</u>, p. 222.

29.   Paul Ricoeur, "Ye Are the Salt of the Earth," in <u>Political and Social Essays by Paul Ricoeur</u>, collected and edited by David Stewart and Joseph Bien (Athens: Ohio University Press, 1974), p. 117.

30.   Ibid., p. 141.

31.   Ibid., p. 70.

32.   Ibid., p. 63.

33.   Ibid., p. 87.

34.   Paul Ricoeur, <u>History and Truth</u>, translated with an introduction by Charles Kelbley (Evanston: Northwestern University Press, 1965), pp. 42-55.

35.   Ricoeur, "Existence and Hermeneutics," in Klemm, p. 202.

knowledge constitutive interests, in Habermas 60

Rerum Novavum, 52
Resurrection, 104
Ricoeur, on hermeneutic of symbolism, x, 106; as an
    integrative framework, xi, 99; arbitration between
    Gadamer and Habermas, 9, 71, 74, 102; on Husserl,
    100; critique of Heidegger, 101; hermeneutical
    phenomenology, 101; hermeneutic of suspicion, 104;
    poetic language, 107; on Moltmann, 108; on Hegel,
    108; on philosophical approximation to kerygma,
    108; on Kantian practical reason, 109, 115; on
    liberation praxis, 111; on democratic socialism,
    111; on humanism, 112; distanciation, 101; on
    Bultman, 105; faith and philosophy, 108; on evil,
    110
Roderick, Rick, critique of Habermas, 70
Rorty, Richard, on Gadamer, 14; on deconstructivism,
    19, 32; critique of Taylor, 30; on Dewey's
    pragmatism, 15; response to charge of nihilism, 32

Saint Thomas Acquinas, 52, 80
Scannone, Juan, 91
scientific discovery, in Polanyi, 46
scientific positivism, in Polanyi, 45
second naivete, in Ricoeur, 107
Segundo, Juan, 91
self interpretation, in Taylor, ix, 20
Sin, in liberation theology, 82, 83
Skinner, B. F., 112
Smith Paul, critique of Foucault, 31; "death of man"
    epistemology, 19, 31
Soelle, Dorothee, 74
Soviet Union, 50
subject referring properties, in Taylor, 20
symbolic meaning, in Ricoeur, 105, 107

Taylor, on praxis, vii; self interpretation, ix, 20,
    34; ethical theory, 23; on Aristotelian logos, 24;
    on deconstructivism, 19; subject referring
    properties, 21; on behavioral science, 21; on
    atomism, 24; designative vs expressive meaning,
    24; on language, 24, 113; critique of Foucault,
    24-27; critique of Rorty, 33; response to
    Connally, 34
Theology of Hope, in Moltmann and Bloch, 108

universal intent, in Polanyi, 41, 47
utopian thinking, 85, 86

Vatian II, 80
violence, in liberation theology, 78, 93, 94

wager, in Ricoeur, 107
Winch, Peter, 66

Zealots, 83